PENGUIN BUSINESS
SMALL IS BIG

Amit Agarwal is a *Teacher* at heart, a *Student* at mind and a *Warrior* in action.

Utilizing this *Student–Teacher–Warrior* mindset, Amit aims to harness and evangelize four life skills: *sales, mindfulness, nutritional diet* and *personal finance*. He believes that incremental progress in harnessing these life skills helps us balance material accomplishments and spiritual growth.

Amit's two books, *The Ultimate Sales Accelerator* and *Small Is Big,* are steps in this journey of evangelizing the four life skills and balancing spirit and matter.

An IIT–IIM alumnus, Amit has professional selling experience in twenty-three countries across bootstrapped and Series A, B, C and D start-ups. He lives in the suburbs of Bengaluru amid beautiful farmlands with his wife, Ayesha, and sons, Tanish and Aarav.

in https://www.linke

✉ amit.agarwal@sale

g www.salespreneur

▶ http://bit.ly/salespreneur_youtube

T0158270

ADVANCE PRAISE FOR THE BOOK

'An incredible book that illustrates the power of "Small is big" with examples from diverse areas such as thoughts, habits, organization culture, communication and productivity. A timely reminder for all of us to harness the power of "small" in business and life'—Hari T.N., head, HR, Bigbasket.com, and author of *From Pony to Unicorn*

'This book is like an hourglass. Every grain of sand emptied builds clear vision on the top. Every page you complete brings clarity in your vision of life. Remember the old adage, 'पुस्तकेषु च या विद्या'—knowledge in a book is not yours until it is read. Go grab your copy and read it ASAP'—G. Sridhar, professor (marketing), Indian Institute of Management Kozhikode

'Amit offers a practical toolkit for use in personal life and business for unlocking higher levels of efficiency and effectiveness. In a world where we are pushed towards more and many, Amit brings out the power of small and few. His easy-to-read style and "learning accelerators" sprinkled through the book can help you start becoming more productive—now!'—Rajesh Jain, managing director, Netcore Solutions Pvt Ltd

'Amit has touched on a very integral change that is happening in this era, reassessing priorities and the importance of letting our values guide our decisions'—Mohamed Adam Wee, chief marketing officer, Manulife Insurance Berhad

'A practical guide to internalizing the big idea of "Small is big" in your daily life and work. Amit has built on his personal experiences to lucidly illustrate the theme, backed up by several examples from the world of business. Easy to read, this book will guide you to "simplify" your life and focus on those few things that will make a big difference'—Praveen Shrikhande, chief digital and information officer, Aditya Birla Fashion and Retail Ltd

'Achieving goals requires focus, and focus requires changes in habits. Even a small yet sustained change can go a long way in delivering significant impact. The book focuses on this simple yet powerful point with a strong narrative from real-life examples. A must-read for anyone aspiring for personal and professional success'—Seshadri D.V.R., clinical professor of marketing, Indian School of Business

'Amit has questioned conventional wisdom with a counter-intuitive book about the importance of sweating the small stuff in our lives and in our careers. Small decisions, small steps, small gestures, small kindnesses. They aren't small. Get small and get going!'—Atul Jalan, CEO and MD, Algonomy, and author of *Where Will Man Take Us*

'The book touches on various insights into productivity and none more important than the power of doing the basics right through self-transformation, which in turn helps one gain both personal and private victory. It's a highly recommended read with tools of self-reflection and lots of soul-searching to unlock one's potential'—Saurabh Kalra, chief operating officer, McDonald's India (W&S)

'The infinite begins with the infinitesimal. If you do not believe in the power of the small, try going to bed with a virus inside your body. Amit Agarwal's work is a profound reminder of the power and impact of small interventions in thoughts, habits, culture, productivity and organization. This book is timely and timeless at the same time!'—Prof. Debashis Chatterjee, author of *Timeless Leadership*

SMALL IS
BIG

*The **Source Code** for*

FULFILMENT, PRODUCTIVITY
& EXTRAORDINARY RESULTS

AMIT AGARWAL

BUSINESS

An imprint of Penguin Random House

PENGUIN BUSINESS

USA | Canada | UK | Ireland | Australia
New Zealand | India | South Africa | China

Penguin Business is part of the Penguin Random House group of companies
whose addresses can be found at global.penguinrandomhouse.com

Published by Penguin Random House India Pvt. Ltd
4th Floor, Capital Tower 1, MG Road,
Gurugram 122 002, Haryana, India

First published in Penguin Business by Penguin Random House India 2022

ISBN 9780143454946

Typeset in Aldine401 BT by MAP Systems, Bengaluru, India

www.penguin.co.in

This book is dedicated to

my teachers,

my wife, Ayesha

and

my sons, Tanish and Aarav

*for being a source of constant inspiration to me and for being my
partners in discovering the infinitely Big in the infinitely Small!*

My Wish for You

Thank you for choosing this book.
May this book help you:

- find purpose and joy in little things.
- embrace what is meaningful and remove the clutter in your life.
- say YES to the priorities that truly matter and NO to everything insignificant.

This is the essence of *Small Is Big*. When you harness 'Small is big', *fulfilment*, *productivity* and *extraordinary results* are inevitable.

Contents

PART III: 'Small Is Big': Fuelling Productivity

Prologue

How Silence and Pain Led the Way

The journey began on an ordinary Sunday. On 6 January 2018, I was at a meditation retreat. Surrounded by almost 300 people, I was unaware that a fantastic, life-changing experience was awaiting me. Isn't this true for most experiences that have the power to alter a person's life completely? They occur at moments when we least expect them. So, what happened on that remarkable day?

I had commenced 2018 by attending an intensive four-day course on advanced meditation. During the entire duration of the course, the participants had to practise silence, barring one segment when we could verbally express ourselves.

On the third day we performed a unique exercise called 'meditation in motion'. Since this was my ninth advanced course, I was well aware of this particular section. But just the thought of it sent shivers down my spine. With great fear in my mind, I began the twenty-minute exercise.

Sitting cross-legged, I had to extend both my arms outwards. Throughout the exercise, they had to be straight. At no point could I bend my arms, not even one little inch. I started to lower my extended arms so that they almost touched the floor. Then, for the next 10 minutes, I had to keep them raised above my shoulders. Once the arms are raised, the last 10 minutes of the exercise are devoted to bringing them down. A teacher was present to guide us through the movements. At every intermediate position, he instructed us to hold our posture for a few seconds.

You must be wondering—why should the simple act of moving my arms up and down send shivers down my spine? My friends, it may sound simple, but it is nothing short of harrowing. Excruciating is the right word to describe the pain. How often have you heard more than 300 people shouting, chanting and crying in pain? That is what was happening in the room. Of course, this pain has a greater purpose. It is to achieve holistic wellness.

It is said that three kinds of pain score very high on the intensity spectrum. They are labour pain, kidney stone pain and a wisdom tooth ache. I have experienced the second and the third. However, the agony I felt during 'meditation in motion' had a similar or maybe even higher intensity than the kidney stone pain and toothache. The only difference was that I had chosen to feel this pain; it was a voluntary decision.

In that state of intense anguish, I thought to myself, *'What can I do right now to increase my commitment towards completing the exercise and minimize the extreme discomfort?'* This old habit of mine, of always asking questions, has benefited me greatly—because questions always create new possibilities and participation.

Immediately, the Universe answered, '*Divide the 20 minutes into sections of one minute each. Dedicate your entire focus to completing that one minute.*'

Armed with this insight, I happily took charge of the situation and concentrated on getting through each minute. Once that minute was over, I started afresh.

What happened after that was incredible. I was able to complete every minute with much greater ease than earlier. Unlike my companions, I was not crying or shouting in pain. In the previous eight courses that I had attended, I had vocally expressed my pain. Suddenly, it had all changed. All I had to do was divide those 20 minutes into small one-minute intervals. With the completion of each interval, I received a boost of confidence. Discomfort became easier to manage. My smile became wider. That one SMALL step of breaking 20 minutes into shorter phases helped me achieve an arduous task. It transformed that painful exercise into a BIG experience and taught me precious lessons in innovation, confidence and fulfilment.

In this state, where I managed to feel a sense of fulfilment and resourcefulness in a challenging situation, the seed for *Small Is Big* was sown. Since 6 January 2018, I started incorporating this principle in all aspects of my life, whether personal, professional or spiritual. And the more I began following the principle of 'Small is big', the more I noticed a similar pattern in how multinational organizations, world leaders and people live their lives, conduct themselves and make critical decisions.

I realized that 'Small is big' is the universal source code for achieving *fulfilment, productivity* and *extraordinary results.* The observations that I made watered the sapling. Finally, what resulted was the fruit, which is this book. 'Small is big' is a revelation, a profound way of life, which I want to share with the world. For this reason, I decided to pen down my thoughts on how we can leverage the source code to bring about a significant and positive difference in the three significant areas of our worldly existence: *life, business* and *productivity.*

May this fruit, my book, enrich every *small* aspect of your life, resulting in a *big* transformation for you.

> *'Be faithful in small things because it is in*
> *them that your strength lies.'*
>   —Mother Teresa

PART I

'Small Is Big'
Transforming Life

1

How Focusing on One Small Thing Helped Me Crack the IIT Entrance Test!

'The successful warrior is the average man, with laser-like focus.'

—Bruce Lee, actor, director, martial artist

Soon after my experience at the retreat I attempted to adopt the 'Small is big' source code in all aspects of my life. Often, my curious mind wondered, *'Is this an approach I have adopted before, perhaps unknowingly? Has "Small is big" always been a part of my life, or it is only now that I am aware of it?'*

To my surprise, the answer was yes! Looking back on my life's milestones, I realized that the experiences that had changed my life forever had resulted from following the idea of 'Small is big'. I didn't know it then.

I grew up in Jhansi, a small and historical city in northern India. My family belonged to a large business community. My father was the only member who worked in an organization; he was employed in a bank. My parents gave my siblings and me an excellent education at convent schools. When I was in the twelfth grade, all my friends prepared for the coveted Indian Institute of Technology (IIT) entrance examination. However, my approach wasn't the same as that of my peers. The idea of studying for school exams and preparing for the IIT entrance test at the same time didn't appeal to me. I focused my energies solely on doing well in the twelfth-grade examinations, and it yielded great results. I scored excellent marks and ranked third in the district. My parents were ecstatic. I still remember my father returning early from work and distributing sweets in the neighbourhood.

Now that I had scored exceptional marks in my examinations, it was time to focus on cracking the IIT entrance exams. Since professional tutoring options were non-existent in Jhansi, I thought of shifting to a bigger town. In July 1993, I moved to Kanpur to train for the exams in an IIT-entrance exam coaching centre. But it wasn't a rosy picture. At age seventeen, I couldn't adjust to being alone in the city. I missed the comfort and warmth of my home and family. I missed home-cooked food, and cooking by myself was hard! All of this put together made studying in Kanpur difficult. In August I returned to Jhansi and enrolled in a correspondence course run by Vidya Mandir Classes, an institute that prepared students for IIT entrance exams. The classes were taught by three brothers who had made it to IIT.

I put my heart and soul into my studies, clocking 12 hours a day and completing all my assignments. While preparing for competitive exams, students often find themselves confused by the sheer volume of material available. Each student follows their own approach. Each teacher recommends something different. However, rather than focusing on many books, I followed what was being taught in the Vidya Mandir classes. And, honestly, I was enjoying this single-minded focus.

Alongside regular teaching, the centre offered face-to-face interactions for the students with the faculty so that they could improve their preparation. These interactions took place in Delhi, and it was during one such interaction that I learned something that single-handedly changed my style of preparation. I am not exaggerating when I say that was the reason I could crack the exam.

The teacher asked the students, 'Out of 300 marks, how much do you need to score to guarantee yourself a spot in IIT?'

Most of the students present were under the impression that you needed very high marks. The majority of us said we needed to score greater than 200. That's pretty high! It was then that the teacher corrected us and revealed something so profound. He said, *To get through the IIT entrance exams, you only need to score 100 out of 300.'*

All of us were shocked. Only 100 out of 300? That is just 33 per cent! We all grew up believing that a good student scores more than 80 per cent in their examinations. That was our definition of success. Suddenly, we were told that 33 per cent could get us through one of India's most challenging and prestigious exams. How was that even possible?

The teacher patiently explained how the nature of the exam is very different from that of the traditional tests students are accustomed to in school. There are around 2000 seats in IIT. The toppers may score above 200. But to crack the exam itself, all a student needs is to cross 100 out of 300 marks. Until that day I had been preparing for the exam in a particular manner, but this revelation impacted me intensely, and I altered my strategy: *I only focused on scoring more than 100.*

Accordingly, I tweaked my preparation. I analysed my strengths and prioritized specific topics and sections. My focus was on mathematics, followed by organic chemistry (inorganic chemistry was not my cup of tea) and, finally, select topics in physics. I studied sample papers to better gauge the question patterns. For every mock exam I appeared for, I scored more than 100. I was satisfied with my progress and confident of the results. Sometimes a friend would tell me about other books, courses and tips to achieve even higher scores. I will be honest—once in a while I would feel sceptical about my strategy and a little disturbed. In those moments, I remembered the words, *'To get through the IIT entrance exams, you only need to score 100 out of 300.'*

I appeared for my IIT entrance exam in April 1994. Many asked me how it went. I had a simple answer to that question, 'I will score 100+.'

I distinctly remember the day the results were published. I was with my friends Rohit and Dinesh.

Soon we were joined by Vivek, another of our friends. He had arrived with a newspaper in his hand.

The second he arrived, he said . . . in fact, almost shouted, 'Amit, what is your roll number?'

'Roll number?' I fumbled.

'*Arre,* your IIT exam roll number.'

The time seemed too short for asking questions or feeling any emotion. I gave Vivek my roll number and he quickly scanned the newspaper.

'Amit, *tera ho gaya IIT mein!* You've cleared the exam!' Vivek exclaimed joyfully.

At that moment I couldn't believe what Vivek had said. It took a little while for the news to sink in. After receiving congratulations from my friends, I cycled back home as fast as I could.

Then occurred one of the most memorable moments of my life. And every time I remember that special day I can see every little detail sparkle before my eyes. When I reached home, my mother was in the kitchen, cooking. From the small opening in our kitchen that looked into the house I could see my father at his prayers in the adjoining room. I didn't want to disturb him.

Gently, I broke the news to my mother, 'Mummy, *mera IIT mein ho gaya* (I have made it to IIT).'

Immediately, her face lit up. The joy and satisfaction etched on her face are hard to describe in words. My father heard me. Between his prayers, he looked at me and smiled. His smile conveyed a lot: blessings, happiness and gratitude.

Can the cracking of one exam by one member bring a family so much joy? It sure did. And all of this happened because of that one *small* piece of advice—*'To get through the IIT entrance exams, you only need to score 100 out of 300.'*

IIT changed my life. It was not just due to the perks that came from studying in such a prestigious institution. I remember my college days as full of fun, laughter and, above all, invaluable learning. For that I am incredibly grateful to the teacher at the coaching class who shared his wisdom about the minimum score needed to pass the entrance examination; and above all to the Universe, for showing me the Big power hidden in Small things.

Can only a single thought—of achieving 100 out of 300 marks—be so unbelievably powerful? Can it help a student crack one of the country's most prestigious exams and bring his parents so much joy? Yes, our thoughts are incredible pockets of power. They can sharpen our focus; they can also strengthen our will or distract us from our path. For that reason, it is vital that we understand and acknowledge the strength of every thought. In the next chapter, we'll explore how powerful a *single* thought can be—in either positively or negatively shaping our lives.

2

The Journey of a Single Thought

*'We are what we think. All that we are arises with our thoughts.
With our thoughts, we make the world.'*

—Buddha

S ince time immemorial, great philosophers have spoken about the influence of our thoughts on our lives. Lao Tzu said:

'Watch your thoughts; they become words. Watch your words; they become actions. Watch your actions; they become a habit. Watch your habits; they become character. Watch your character; it becomes your destiny.'

Now, if I say, 'Our entire life is the totality of our thoughts and habits', does this statement resonate with you? If we think of our mind as akin to a beautiful garden, then:

• Our *positive thoughts are the seeds* that will grow and beautify the garden.

- Our *negative thoughts are the weeds* that require removal.
- Our *habits are like the water and fertilizer* that will foster an environment of growth for the seeds.

We begin by addressing the negative thoughts, the weeds in our beautiful garden. Have you ever wondered why a single thought can be so powerful? That is because it never exists in isolation. You can never ponder upon only one idea. *A chain reaction accompanies every single thought.* Here are a few examples:

Thought 1

I have to become a great presenter.
Thoughts that follow in reaction:

- It will help me in making impactful business presentations.
- Which courses can I attend?
- How about storytelling or public speaking?
- Should I sign up for an online class or an offline class?
- How do I manage my busy schedule and find time for the class?
- Do I have the resources to fund this course right now?

Thought 2

I require a raise in my salary.
Thoughts that follow in reaction:

- It has been years since I have received a substantial increase.

- My manager is not able to understand my situation.
- I see my company hiring new employees and giving them handsome increments.
- This isn't fair.
- The culture is not correct.
- I want to resign.

Thought 3

My kids spend too much time playing video games.
Thoughts that follow in reaction:

- It is harmful to their holistic well-being.
- They hardly listen and exceed the agreed duration every time.
- I see them becoming quite aggressive and more undisciplined.
- Shall I send them to a boarding school?
- But how will my wife and I live without our kids?
- How will the children live without us?

You will realize from these examples how a chain reaction emanates from just one thought. Thus, it becomes critical to learn how to calm our minds and watch our positive and negative thoughts and feelings. In his iconic book *As You Think,* James Allen wrote, 'Every thought-seed sown or allowed to fall into the mind, and to take root there, produces its own, blossoming sooner or later into the act, and bearing its fruits of opportunity and circumstance. Good thoughts bear good fruit. Bad thoughts bear bad fruit.'

So, can you imagine the toxic reaction that negative thoughts have the power to create?

My deals are not closing. Am I any good?

These people mocked me. I want to hit them.

My partner betrayed me. My life is over.

A cynical world view can leave a severe and long-lasting impression on a person's mind. It creates a sense of finality, leaving one feeling that everything is about to end. It seems as if nothing is in your control. We must address such thoughts and feelings, both at the *conscious* and *subconscious* levels.

There are three ways by which we can alter our negative thoughts consciously:

1. Reframing
2. Practising gratitude
3. Harnessing resourceful memories

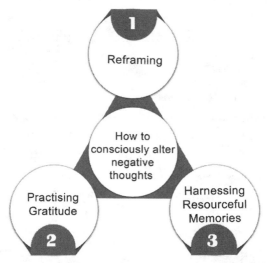

Fig. 2.1: Three ways to alter negative thoughts consciously

We will break down each concept with an example. I'll delve into my own life and share instances of my using these three tactics to change a negative situation into a positive one.

The negative situation: My elder son is shouting at me. Surprised at his sudden outburst, I feel hurt and upset. A part of me wants to shout back at him for his behaviour. An unpleasant situation is brewing. How can I change this tense atmosphere into something that will bring peace and help me understand my son's perspective?

Reframing

Reframing any negative situation enables us to view the given problem from an *alternative* perspective. This perspective opens the door for positive options and opinions to enter one's mind and to change our mindset. You must be thinking: how do I begin to think positively in a situation when I am so stressed? It is simple. Take a moment and ask yourself this question:

What is the positive intention of this situation/person that I need to understand?

As my son was shouting I asked this question of myself, and the following thoughts came to my mind:

Is my son's shouting a reflection of some intense pain he is going through but cannot express?

Is he feeling lonely, unable to meet his friends and enjoy school because of the pandemic?

Is he finding it difficult to cope with a particular problem?

My son shouting at me is an opportunity for me to understand his emotions. Let me sit down and have a calm word with him, I tell myself. Let me connect with my son and find out what is troubling him.

Practising Gratitude

Gratitude can cast a positive light on a negative situation. This is because appreciation is a feeling that comes right from the heart. It is pure and full of joy.

In the same situation with my son, I can ask myself, *'What are three things I am grateful to my son for?'*

I am grateful to my son for helping me relive my childhood. Playing cricket, watching cartoons and vacations are lovely experiences I relive because of my son.

I am grateful to my son for calling me *Daddy*. I don't know why, but it immediately puts a smile on my face and makes me feel so happy.

I am grateful to my son for allowing me to experience the most miraculous event in the universe—the birth of a child—at close hand. Every time I remember it, I get goosebumps.

Harnessing Resourceful Memories

'We are nothing but a bundle of memories. When we harness a positive memory, happiness and joy become inevitable.'
—Amit Agarwal

It often happens that minor, commonplace incidents have the power to give us profound wisdom. One morning in March 2020, I woke up and went downstairs to join my family. My wife was with my children in their bedroom.

After exchanging morning pleasantries with me, my wife asked with a smile, 'Amit, when you think about Tanish, which resourceful memory comes to mind?'

Tanish is my elder son. It was a lovely question, and I pondered for a while before answering. A broad smile appeared on my face as I said:

'I remember that moment when I first held Tanish in my arms. He was a newborn baby, crying loudly. I was looking at him with absolute amazement. Hearing Tanish cry, the nurse remarked, "*What lungs!*" For a moment, *time stood still.* I even forgot you, lying there on the operating table.'

Touched by my answer, my wife urged me to share another resourceful memory for the family to enjoy. I was beginning to enjoy this digging up of fond memories. I remembered another one.

I had just returned from Orlando after a two-day business trip. It was around 6 a.m. When I entered my room I saw six-month-old Tanish lying in his crib. He was awake. The second his bright eyes fell on me, he started making pleasant gurgling sounds and gave me a beautiful smile. It was a wonderful moment. All my exhaustion disappeared at the sight of that smile. Later, I found out that Tanish had been unwell for the last two days. Perhaps the six-month-old baby was missing his father!

As I shared such cherished moments with my family, we felt immense joy and love. The room was full of warmth. Each one of us had a happy smile on our faces. An ordinary morning was transformed into a beautiful memory in a matter of 2 or 3 minutes. All it took was the simple act of sharing a resourceful memory. Harnessing positive memories immediately changes our state of being. We overcome the feeling of being unresourceful or 'not being good enough'. A sense of joy replaces negative thoughts and brings about optimism and positivity.

In the same situation with my son, I can ask:

What positive memories can I harness for Tanish?

Every time I ask this question, the two experiences mentioned above flash in my memory and the anger subsides. Love increases.

So, the next time negative thoughts plague you about a person or situation, ask yourself: *What positive memories can I harness for this person/entity/situation?*

For example:

What positive memories can I harness for my company?
What positive memories can I harness for my manager?
What positive memories can I harness for my spouse?

When you find the answers, I assure you that it will refresh your mind and give you clarity and composure. Leverage your answers to decide what to do about the situation. An anxious mind is a breeding ground for muddled thoughts. When you can control the negativity, it opens pathways that eventually transform your life. All of this can happen by *Reframing*, *Practising Gratitude* and *Harnessing Resourceful Memories*.

Can Water be Affected by Human Thought?*

Dr Masaru Emoto, a Japanese scientist and author of *The Hidden Messages in Water,* set out to answer this unique question. Using high-speed photographs and an advanced technology called magnetic resonance analysis, Dr Emoto observed how water's molecular structure transforms when exposed to human words and thoughts. He discovered that thoughts elicited two kinds of responses in water:

- Positive (loving, benevolent and compassionate) human thoughts resulted in beautiful and pleasing molecular formations.
- Negative (fearful and discordant) human thoughts resulted in disconnected, disfigured and 'unpleasant' molecular formations.

Please visit these links to view the photographs showing the water crystals reacting to words like 'Evil', 'Thank you', 'Love and Gratitude' and 'You Disgust Me':

- https://thewellnessenterprise.com/emoto/
- https://www.masaru-emoto.net/en/crystal-2/

---

* Masaru Emoto—Office Masaru Emoto. (n.d.). Accessed 19 March 2021, https://www.masaru-emoto.net/en/masaru/; 'Dr Masaru Emoto and Water Consciousness,' The Wellness Enterprise, accessed 28 February 2021, https://thewellnessenterprise.com/emoto/

Negative words and phrases like 'Evil' or 'You disgust me' result in unpleasant formations.

Positive words like 'Thank you' and 'Love and Gratitude' lead to pleasant formations.

The Wellness Enterprise website also shows another set of photographs of water molecules from the Fujiwara Dam. They were taken *before* and *after* Reverend Kato Hoki, the chief priest of Jyuhouin Temple, offered an hour-long prayer over the water. You can see the remarkable difference in the structure of the molecules. The first pattern of molecules looks disturbed, almost aggressive. The second photograph exudes calm and warmth.

Thanks to Dr Masaru Emoto's experimental work, we can look at water and its frozen crystals to realize the healing power in positive thinking, uplifting speech and prayer. Now, you must be thinking, how is this scientific research connected to our lives?

We all know that approximately 60 per cent of the human body consists of water. Merging this knowledge and Dr Emoto's study on how water molecules react to human intention, can we say that our thoughts, words and motives determine our body's molecular formations? If our bodies are 60 per cent water, imagine the contribution of positive and negative thoughts to what is happening inside us.

Learning Accelerator

1. Think of a situation where you felt distressed and uncomfortable. Acknowledge your feelings. If you think that writing is better, pen down your thoughts in the space below.

   _____

   _____

   _____

2. Now, using the power of Reframing, Practising Gratitude and Harnessing Resourceful Memories, attempt to rethink and alter your previous approach to the situation.

   • Reframing:

     _____

     _____

     _____

   • Practising Gratitude:

     _____

     _____

     _____

• Harnessing Resourceful Memories:

_____

_____

_____

3. Check your new-found state and identify the difference in perspective.

_____

_____

_____

Many of you must be wondering if all three steps are required. Honestly, it depends on the intensity of the situation and your emotional state. Start with Reframing, then move on to explore Gratitude and Resourceful Memories if the situation calls for a more in-depth and intensive approach.

This section was focused on inducing a transformation by *consciously* changing our negative thoughts into positive ones. Is there a way to bring about such changes *subconsciously*?

For that, let's step into the world of habits in the following chapter.

3

Micro-habits and their Associated Domino Effect

'If you are going to achieve excellence in big things,
you develop the habit in little matters. Excellence is
not an exception, it is a prevailing attitude.'

—Colin Powell, 65th secretary of state, USA

How do you define the word 'habit'?

According to the Cambridge dictionary, 'A habit is something that you do often and regularly, sometimes *without knowing* that you are doing it.'

The Merriam-Webster dictionary says, 'Habit is an acquired mode of behaviour that has become nearly or completely *involuntary*.'

You might wonder why I chose to begin the chapter with a definition of 'habit' from the dictionary, and I will explain.

When I found these definitions, two phrases stood out for me. You follow a habit *without knowing* that you are doing so, or *nearly or completely involuntarily*. Isn't this worthy of reflection? Almost every moment, we perform an action that we have become so accustomed to doing that we are not even aware of it!

Take a moment and recall the time you sleep and wake up every day. Is there a pattern to it? What do you do right after you wake up, during the first hour of the day? Do you notice a similarity in what you do every day? Don't be surprised if you do. It is all because many of our activities are simply a matter of habit.

Just as a fun exercise, set a timer the next time you sit down for dinner. Do this for a couple of days. You will be amazed to find a consistent pattern. It will be the same with the number of times we brush our teeth, how we drive, how we talk, the words or expressions we use. There is a pattern, a trend, in each action we perform.

As humans, we are the sum total of our habits.

Habit Versus Addiction

As a term, addiction is often associated with the consumption of harmful substances. The moment someone says 'addiction', our mind goes to alcohol, smoking or drugs. But are addictions only related to substance abuse?

Children spend hours in front of their tablets or computers playing video games.

Teenagers cannot resist social media and feel the need to share every little detail of their lives on it.

Most of us, whether we are teenagers or adults, check our phones every few seconds.

On the surface, social media or video games may not seem to be as dangerous as drugs. But when you think about the number of times a day you are tempted to browse social media or play online games, you will realize that it is as addictive as a toxic substance that is consumed. Most importantly, they are as likely to disturb your mental and social balance as substance abuse does. Trust me, they are equally hard to quit.

In the end, *addictions are harmful habits with alarmingly high repetition rates.* So, whether it is alcohol or spending hours scrolling through social media, the moment you begin to repeat anything too often, you are addicted. There are no two ways about it.

In the following two sections of the chapter, we will delve more deeply into the subject, exploring the nuances of how our habits are created, their impact on our lives, and practical ways in which we can change them for an immense transformation.

Section One

What Makes a Habit?

The Habit-Formation Process

Simply, habits consist of *repetition* of an act. Repetition, in turn, is the result of many factors.

Family

I have travelled in around forty countries and spent five years working in the USA. Yet, I have maintained strict vegetarian food habits. How is that possible? That's because I was born into a vegetarian family, and since my childhood I have only eaten a certain kind of food.

After attending a naturopathy workshop, my father started practising a yoga posture called Vajrasana. To improve digestion, this yoga posture has to be done after eating food. Every day after food, he would sit in vajrasana or diamond pose. Seeing him, I started doing vajrasana after having my meals. It has been around 30 years. Now it is a habit.

Besides food habits and wellness practices, the family is a formative influence in shaping one's language of communication, religious beliefs and routine lifestyle. The way we have been brought up has a significant role in how we live our lives.

Friends

After family, friends play an essential role in moulding one's behaviour. This behaviour, when repeated, forms a habit.

I am often surprised when my children address one another as 'dude' or use the phrase 'What's up?' I realize that they have probably picked this up from their friends in the residential community or school.

Interaction with friends not only influences our language but also our decisions, hobbies and lifestyle. Most children enjoy playing video games. If you notice, there is a particular time when all their friends come online for multi-player games. More than the game itself, they are driven by a psychological urge to feel a sense of participation and inclusion. Especially in the pandemic era, video games became virtual meeting spaces for children who felt lonely in their homes. As parents, we did not oppose it because it gave our children a sense of belonging. Unfortunately, addiction to video games has become a harmful habit that we must address in a phased manner.

Societal and Cultural Customs

The larger societal and cultural space we live in impacts our way of thinking.

As an Indian, I greet a person with folded hands, saying 'namaste'. If I meet someone much older, I touch their feet as a gesture of respect and seek their blessings. When you travel to Indonesia, will you find the same behaviour? Of course not. In Indonesia, people meet each other and say 'selamat (peace)' with a slight nod of the head.

Similarly, families have a particular way of celebrating a festival. In my home, the primary festival is Diwali. We light lamps, burst crackers and gorge on a delicious sweet called gujiya. My sons and I wait all year for Diwali just so that we can eat that sweet. This has become our habit. You'll find the same practices in your family. Take any festival which you celebrate at home. There is a pattern in which you enjoy the occasion, how you decorate your house, what you love to eat and so on. Some of the activities mentioned above may appear as rituals, *The point to note is that rituals, when repeated, form habits*. The key word in habit formation is 'repetition'. Realizing the power of repetition, our ancestors created many festivals to cultivate the habit of celebrating the goodness and positivity in our lives.

Media

I use media as an umbrella term for the different kinds of content we are consuming. The most popular formats include newspapers, films, television, video games and social media. Are they capable of forming habits in their consumers? Yes, they are. The kind of content we enjoy and the amount of time we spend on different media platforms impact our lifestyle, thoughts and even talking style! When the patterns are repeated, they become a habit.

Think about the following:

What kind of content am I watching/reading/listening to repeatedly?

How many hours a day am I on social media?

How often do I feel the urge to check my phone?

When you begin to answer these questions, you will find a consistent pattern in the way you are engaging with media. There is a similarity in what you watch every day, how often you check your messages and the time you spend on media. The first thing many people do on waking up is to check their messages, whether on WhatsApp or another platform. Others read the newspaper. That has become a habit. That is the first thing they do every morning, day in and day out.

Let me share an example of how media consumption created a habit.

I started watching the YouTube channel of the Satvic movement,[1] a non-profit educational platform for wellness and nutrition, which has over 3 million subscribers. Two of the videos inspired me to take action—one about ash gourd (white pumpkin) juice and another about

---

[1] www.satvicmovement.org, https://youtube.com/c/SatvicMovement.

intermittent fasting. Now, drinking ash gourd juice daily and 14 to 16 hours of intermittent fasting has become a habit for me.

Let me share another experience. Aarav, my younger son, uses a term 'OP' every time he wishes to express his happiness. 'Mamma, the pickle you made is OP.' 'Daddy, the reclining seating in this movie theatre is OP.' 'Honey (his elder brother's pet name), this new video game is OP.'

Curiously, I asked Aarav, 'What does OP mean?'

He said, 'Over Powering.'

Wanting to learn more, I asked, 'From where did you learn this word OP?'

Immediately he said, 'YouTube.'

You could say that his habit of watching YouTube has contributed to his vocabulary, in a way.

Environmental Factors

The environment in which we live has the power to form habits in us. A person can develop a habit in response to their professional, personal and spiritual surroundings.

The best example of this is the COVID-19 pandemic, which has inspired incredible changes in how offices and schools function daily.

Globally, companies and employees warmed up to the idea of everyone working from home. It is a game changer, as organizations now realize that business objectives can be met even when teams operate from their homes. This has been a revelation, and it took a pandemic to change the habit and mindset that corporate goals can *only* be accomplished in offices.

Simultaneously, buyers and sellers are dabbling in virtual selling models such as online meetings, demos and discussions rather than meeting in person. Gone are the days when teams required a physical venue to meet and brainstorm. The adoption of virtual selling has created a habit of completing the entire sales cycle remotely.

Even the education system had to move from physical classes to online courses on Zoom and Google Meet platforms. However, a drawback is the increased screen time for children.

Let me share a personal anecdote about how the professional environment engenders habits.

In 2002, I was working for Cognizant Technologies. I was serving a client in Greenbay, Wisconsin. Working as a project manager was new to me, and I was enjoying the experience. The client had three software production releases every year, that is, once every four months. On the first day of the project initiation, we had to schedule all review meetings in advance for four months. This entailed setting up nearly ten to fifteen reviews for every project to manage reviewers' availability during the short review cycles.

Moreover, we had to send content 48 hours before the meetings to ensure productive interactions. The client's requirements enabled me to develop a great habit. Even today, I send content for a meeting or event well in advance. It is something that I enjoy doing, and it ensures fruitful discussions.

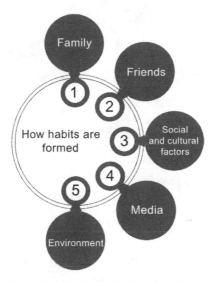

Fig. 3.1: The Five Factors behind Habit Formation

What drives repetition?

Previously, we briefly touched upon the fact that habits are formed as a result of repetition. But what is the drive behind this repetition? What prompts us humans to repeat an action so often that it becomes a habit? The answer is *Risk and/or Reward*. A pattern is formed because our brain looks to mitigate risk and/or gain reward through repetition.

**Fig. 3.2: The Three Rs of Habit Formation:
Reward, Risk and Repetition**

The table below shows examples of habits and the associated reward/risk mitigation triggers.

Habit	Reward	Risk (of not doing it)
Celebrating Christmas	Cake, family time and gifts	
Waking up at 5 a.m.	More time for exercise, reading, meditation and writing	
Playing video games	The instant joy of participation	Feeling left out
Quitting smoking	Healthy body and mind	Vulnerability to cancer and other illnesses
Following the sales process	Better conversions and gaining the trust of the management	Lower conversion rates and strained relationship with management

How long does it take for a habit to form?

In the 1950s, a plastic surgeon called Maxwell Maltz noticed that his patients required twenty-one days to adjust to a new reality, such as a reconstructed face or an amputated leg. In 1960, he published his findings in a bestselling book called *Psycho-Cybernetics*. It sold nearly 30 million copies and is the origin of the widespread belief that it takes twenty-one days to form a habit.[2]

---

[2] J. Clear, 'How Long Does it Actually Take to Form a New Habit? (Backed by Science)', https://jamesclear.com/new-habit.

The twenty-one-day theory was broken in 2009, when the *European Journal of Social Psychology* published another study on the topic. Phillipa Lally and her team from University College, London, conducted in-depth research on habit formation by observing ninety-six volunteers over twelve weeks. Lally's team discovered that, on average, it took sixty-six days to form a habit. The broad range of variation was from 19 days to 254 days. One of their more positive findings was that if a person missed a day while developing a new habit, it did not materially impact the habit-formation process.[3]

---

[3] 'Need to Form a New Habit? Give Yourself at least 66 Days', PsychCentral, https://psychcentral.com/blog/need-to-form-a-new-habit-66-days.

Section Two

Micro-Habits Make Macro-Changes

All this while you may have been wondering, 'All right, I understand the importance of habits. But how are they connected to "Small is big"? What is the relation?'

For now, allow me to answer this question using a simple statement.

Small changes in habits lead to big results.

The meaning of this statement will become clearer as I share personal experiences that illustrate it.

I once had a habit, and I think it is familiar to almost every second person globally—I felt the urge to check my phone at *very short intervals*. It distracted me from whatever I was doing, and by the end of the day the increased screen time led to utter exhaustion. Often, I felt disconnected from my surroundings but more connected to what was happening on my phone. I realized that my checking the phone was entirely out of unconscious habit. It wasn't that there was something urgent on my phone that needed attention.

I admitted to myself, 'Yes, I am addicted to my phone. How can I change this?'

The most-used applications on my phone are my email account, WhatsApp and LinkedIn. Can I delete them? No, I cannot do that at any cost. So, I decided to disable my notifications. This *small* change worked wonders. I was able to concentrate better. My screen time was considerably reduced. But the story doesn't end here.

In January 2020, I came across an interview with Cal Newport, author of *Deep Work*. He said, *'Social media is like giving a cigarette to a thirteen-year-old.'*

What a hard-hitting and truthful statement. It impacted me immensely.

As a solution, Cal recommends quitting social media. While it is a fascinating and enticing thought, I didn't think I was ready for such a significant step. I had to find a middle ground. So, I decided that I would completely distance myself from all kinds of social media every Saturday. It meant that I would not be checking WhatsApp, LinkedIn, Facebook and Instagram that day of the week.

In the beginning it wasn't easy. I was tempted to take a little peek, but I controlled my urge to check my phone and persisted with my resolve. Suddenly, I had more time on Saturdays. I could play cricket on the terrace with my sons, an activity we never did before. I cooked at least one or two meals for my family. That simple change gave my wife more time to relax. We would go to the movies and for lunch. Some Saturdays I practise meditation and observing silence till 12.30 p.m. I began video-calling my parents frequently and had more time to write. Both activities gave me an immense sense of fulfilment.

Just by disabling notifications and not checking social media on Saturdays, many different things were getting done and bringing me so much joy. I was experiencing the 'domino effect', a phenomenon where one event sets off a chain of events, resulting in a cumulative effect. To understand the domino effect, start by lining dominos at an equal distance from each other. Gently tap the first domino. Observe how all the other dominoes fall just from your lightly tapping the first domino.

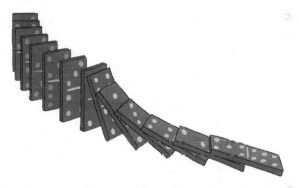

Fig. 3.3: The Domino Effect

In his YouTube video,[4] which has more than 13 million views, Stephen Morris has captured the power of the domino effect. Morris placed thirteen dominos in a line, each 1.5 times larger than the previous one. The first domino was very small, just 5 mm high and 1 mm thick. The thirteenth domino weighed 100 pounds and stood more than a metre tall. By tapping the smallest domino,

---

[4] S. Morris, 'Domino Chain Reaction (Geometric Growth in Action)', 5 October 2009. https://www.youtube.com/watch?v=y97rBdSYbkg.

the subsequent twelve dominoes, including the largest one, fell. Morris remarks that if he had increased the number of dominoes to twenty-nine, the last domino would have been the size of the Empire State Building.

If we think of the simple act of abstaining from social media one day of the week as the smallest domino, we can see how a micro-habit can bring about such a significant change. Just the way the gentle tapping of a domino only 5 mm high and 1 mm thick can make the largest domino weighing 100 pounds fall, a single micro-habit has the power to make a profound difference in our lives.

Can You Change the World By Making Your Bed?

In 2014, Naval Adm. William H. McRaven, the ninth commander of US Special Operations Command, was invited to deliver the university-wide commencement speech at the University of Texas at Austin. His speech went viral, and today has more than 12 million views on YouTube. One of the principles for success shared by Naval Adm. McRaven was 'Make your Bed'. Here is an excerpt from his speech:

'Every morning in basic SEAL training, my instructors, who at the time were all Vietnam veterans, would show up in my barracks room and the first thing they would inspect was your bed. If you did it right, the corners would be square, the covers pulled tight, the pillow centred just under the

headboard and the extra blanket folded neatly at the foot of the rack—that's Navy talk for bed.

'It was a simple task—mundane at best. But every morning we were required to make our bed to perfection. It seemed a little ridiculous at the time, particularly in light of the fact that we were aspiring to be real warriors, tough battle-hardened SEALs, but the wisdom of this simple act has been proven to me many times over.

'If you make your bed every morning, you will have accomplished the first task of the day. It will give you a small sense of pride, and it will encourage you to do another task and another and another. By the end of the day, that one task completed will have turned into many tasks completed. **Making your bed will also reinforce the fact that little things in life matter. If you can't do the little things right, you will never do the big things right.**

'And, if by chance you have a miserable day, you will come home to a bed that is made—that you made—and a made bed gives you encouragement that tomorrow will be better.

'If you want to change the world, start off by making your bed.'

How to Create Micro-Habits

Small changes in habits create a domino effect.
The changes may appear as just minor tweaks of your old ways, but the continuous impact they have is brilliant.

So, how do we create effective micro-habits? I'll begin by sharing a straightforward and accessible framework.

STEP 1:
Choose one pillar from the following:

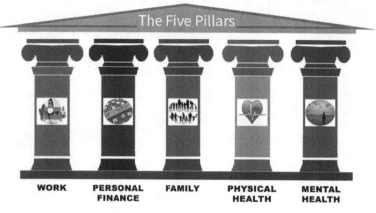

Fig. 3.4

STEP 2:
Under that pillar, list all the problems that you are currently experiencing. From that list, circle the *top three issues* you wish to address.

STEP 3:
List all the benefits you will enjoy if you manage to tackle all the problems for the pillar chosen in the preceding step. This will help you to experience the nature of your desired state. Choose the *three most important benefits.*

STEP 4:
For each of the elements identified in Step 2 and Step 3, what is *the one thing that you can START and/or STOP doing?*

STEP 5:
Make that change and continue repeating that action for sixty-six days until it becomes a habit.

An example will make the steps easier to grasp:
Step 1: Choosing from the five pillars.
- I choose Physical Health.

Step 2: Identifying the problems I am facing regarding my physical health and selecting the three most important ones.
- A feeling of extreme exhaustion in the evening, probably due to too much screen time
- Digestive problems
- Disturbed sleep; pale, tired-looking skin

Step 3: Listing the benefits I wish to enjoy and the characteristics of my desired state.
- Energetic body and mind
- Better digestion
- Healthy, radiant skin

Step 4: Finding out what I can *start doing and/or stop doing* to tackle my health issues and achieve my goals.

START:
- Intermittent fasting (a dietary practice where a person fasts for 14 to 16 hours in the day)
- Drinking white pumpkin (also known as ash gourd) juice every morning

STOP:
- Direct consumption of milk

Step 5: Making the change and continuing it for sixty-six days.

Final Result: I started my micro-changes in the last week of November 2020. By the end of January 2021, both my Start and Stop actions had become habits!

The 3-inch Journey

What is the tongue? It is a muscular organ, roughly three inches long, and enables humans to taste. What is taste? Taste is a sensory experience. Most importantly, it is a deciding factor when it comes to what we eat. We form our food habits depending on what the tongue perceives as tasty. Therefore, it wouldn't be incorrect to say that just a small three-inch organ in the vast human body governs our likes and dislikes regarding food. Be it a pizza or an apple, the food needs to only traverse a three-inch passage before its taste becomes non-existent. After that, we cannot experience its flavour.

Isn't it fascinating? A short passage and, post that, taste ceases to be. There is a famous proverb: *'You are what you eat.'* Imagine what could happen if we choose our food wisely rather than succumbing to the cravings of the three-inch tongue. Imagine the possibilities for our health and well-being it will open. This humbling thought can help us become more mindful of what we choose to eat. It can go a long way in making us healthier eaters who prioritize balanced nutrition and physical well-being over taste.

As in the above scenario, you can develop micro-habits in response to the challenges you are experiencing in any of the five pillars of life. By starting with one valuable micro-practice *and/or* stopping another practice that doesn't contribute to your well-being, significant changes can be ensured in life.

Let me share a few examples of the micro-habits I developed in the five pillars of my life and their domino effects that I experienced, enriching my personal, professional and spiritual life.

Work

Problem: The COVID-19 pandemic saw the majority of the workforce working remotely, and one of the most significant drawbacks of this was the blurring of personal and professional lives. Work-from-home led to a considerable increase in my working hours and screen time. Not only was I completely drained, but I also didn't have any time for my family. A healthy and wholesome work-life balance was becoming more difficult to achieve than before.

My START micro-habit: I began to work in a way that would enable me to finish my professional deliverables by 6.30 p.m. Since repetition creates a habit, I persisted with this for the next sixty-six days until this working style became one. Now my style has been auto-tuned to get all my tasks completed by the cut-off time organically. My evenings are spent with my family, on activities that bring joy and peace.

Personal finance

Problem: For the longest time, my financial state was akin to that of a leaking bucket placed under a steady stream of water. While my earnings were decent, my savings were very low. The corpus in my saving accounts had remained stagnant for a long time. At the same time, very high EMIs were denting my reserves. Financially, I was distressed. It impacted my mental state. I felt trapped.

My START micro-habit: In 2016, I made a conscious choice to plan better and enhance my savings. I created an automated fixed deposit and a monthly SIP (Systematic Investment Plan) to strengthen my savings position. They were small decisions but went a long way in teaching me the importance of planning. Micro-habit, macro-impact!

My STOP micro-habit: My father was a bank employee and used to take loans for many things.

Subconsciously influenced by him, I also developed the habit of taking on debt. At one time, I had six loans. I somehow closed four loans but two of them were amounting to Rs 1,20,000 in monthly payments.

In 2018, I decided to end the crippling pressure I felt because of these two massive loans. I spoke to my wife and together, we decided to sell our house in Hyderabad. It was a tough decision, but it was more important to reduce the mental burden I was continually experiencing. Using the funds from the sale of the house, I closed both my loans. The relief I felt is difficult to convey in words.

Transforming my debts made me feel free and fearless. By paying back all six loans, I also stopped my habit of taking on debt.

Family

Problem: Every family enjoys watching television. Of course, it is a fun activity. But, apart from that, I wanted some productive ways in which I could spend more time with my children. Was there a way to bring the family together that did not involve gadgets?

My START micro-habit: As a family, we started adopting the following routines:

We decided to eat dinner together. Every night, without fail.

You must be wondering, 'What is so tough about eating together?' It so happened that initially my children would feel restless during dinner and want to watch television. My wife and I decided to address this innovatively. For dinner, we chose foods that our children enjoyed. We discussed topics that they could relate to. For example, my elder son Tanish is very interested in technology. So, one day we discussed what the ideal new phone for my wife could be. As a result, the children too began appreciating the act of dining together, and a beautiful camaraderie among us grew.

Physical activity became important.

Even after living for two years in our new home, we hardly used our terrace. But the lockdown changed this once and for all. Since my children could no longer play outside, I decided to use our terrace to play cricket! We took our bats, ball and stumps and started daily games. I cannot explain what joy and bonding that the simple act of playing cricket together has brought to our lives. The precious memories we have created bring a smile to my face every time I recall them . . . even as I am writing this!

And, apart from the happiness of spending time together, playing a sport is a great way to develop focus, speed and team spirit.

So, ask yourself, *'Apart from the <usual activity>, what is/ are the <one/three new activities> I can do with my <kids/wife/ parents> and do this <every day/every week>?'*

This one *small* question will lead to many moments of joy. This is the spirit of 'Small is big'.

My STOP micro-habit: As I have written earlier, I stopped working after 6.30 p.m. and made a firm decision to spend evenings with my family. At the same time, my sons agreed to stop checking their iPad after 7.30 p.m. When all the family members meet halfway and decide to adopt a good habit, the changes each one makes become fun and easy.

Physical health

Problem: 'I don't have the time to exercise' is the most common excuse for those who realize they lack exercise but try to avoid doing something about it. Think about it. You send your car for servicing every three to six months. Do you ever consider skipping that? Then, why such apathy when it comes to your body?

My START micro-habit: Over the years, I have made it a habit to include 17–20 minutes of daily exercise. Yes, that is all it takes. Just 20 minutes of your 24 hours. Choose any kind of physical training or sport that you enjoy. I usually cycle, walk or do surya namaskars (sun salutations). A *small* investment goes a long way. It is an investment of just 20 minutes of your day.

Use this risk-reward framework to motivate yourself to start or continue exercising:

If I don't exercise, I will lose:

1. _____

2. _____

3. _____

If I exercise daily, I will gain:

1. _____

2. _____

3. _____

Mental health

Problem: All this while, I have begun describing a problem with a personal challenge that needed to be conquered. Here, I'll begin differently. I'll share a particular childhood memory. When I was a little boy living in Jhansi, we had holy men visiting our home almost every day. I was fascinated by them. I wondered how someone could be so calm, so at peace with their surroundings. My curiosity led me to attend my first Art of Living Course in 1999 and start practising Vipassana in 2018.

There used to be a time when my ambitions made me impatient and exhausted. I wanted to achieve a great number of things and, most importantly, wanted them to happen fast. It made me agitated, always stressed and, in a few situations, quite rude towards others. So, when I found this getting in the way of life, I knew that something had to be done. I have always been driven by a desire to work on myself, to be a better version of myself. Therefore, I had to lose this distortion and put my heart and soul into gaining the 3 Ps: *Peace, Patience* and *Politeness*. My objective was to enhance my emotional intelligence significantly. Emotional intelligence empowers us to be equanimous under both pain and pleasure.

My START micro-habit: In my personal experience, sound mental health and emotional intelligence can be achieved by participating in three profoundly impactful activities: *Meditation, the practice of Gratitude and Self-Talk.*

Meditation

It is believed that when the Buddha was asked by a disciple, 'What did you gain from meditation?' he replied, 'Nothing. Let me tell you what I lost . . . anger, anxiety, depression, insecurity, fear of old age and death.' The Buddha's emphatic reply reminds us that, sometimes, losing is a much more powerful phenomenon than gaining.

Among the various forms of meditation, the simplest form, which I practise, is anapanasati.[5] This method is believed to have been taught by Gautam Buddha himself and is mentioned in several Buddhist texts. Let me break it down for you in the simplest way possible.

---

[5] https://en.wikipedia.org/wiki/Anapanasati.

Ana is the state when your breath enters your nostrils.

Pana is the state when your breath goes out of your nostrils.

Sati means *to be with*.

Anapanasati therefore means *to be with your incoming and outgoing breath*. All you need to do is to be connected to the act of breathing as your breath enters and exits your nostrils. You can start your mediation journey by practising anapanasati, a powerful technique.

When you devote even as little as 20 minutes of your day to meditation, you only consume 1.4 per cent of the 1440 minutes available to you in the day. In the long run, this translates into 10 hours of meditation monthly and 120 hours of meditation yearly!

In fact, this is exactly how I convinced my children to begin meditation. In February 2020, I was attending a three-day Vipassana meditation course. During the onboarding, a teacher told me, 'Mr Amit, meditation is like giving food to your mind.'

I thought, 'What a powerful metaphor!'

That was when a thought came to my mind, 'Can my children start meditating?'

While the idea was fantastic, I wondered if my children would be willing to embrace meditation. As expected, they replied with a big NO!

'Tanish and Aarav, let's do meditation every day.'

'What . . . ' replied Aarav.

'No *waaaay*,' Tanish agreed with his brother.

'Okay. Then let's do it three times a week.'

Once again, both said no. However, this time, the intensity of their refusal was less than the first time.

Nonetheless, I was still concerned about my children not agreeing at all to take up meditation.

'How many minutes are there in a day?' I asked them.

Tanish and Aarav thought for a while, '60 minutes multiplied by 24.'

'Yes, that is 1440 minutes in a day. And how many minutes does each of you need to meditate?'

Tanish and Aarav answered 14 minutes and 11 minutes, respectively. The answers were prompt, because during our time at a meditation centre in Bengaluru, we had learnt that the duration of meditation must be equal to one's age.

'So, 14 minutes and 11 minutes are less than 1 per cent of 1,440 minutes.'

Immediately, I saw a look of surprise on their faces.

'Can you give less than 1 per cent of your day to meditation?'

I could see that my words were making a difference. My children were opening up to the possibility of meditating.

Building on, I said, 'How about we do it every weekend? Just Saturdays and Sundays?'

Both agreed immediately. Since July 2020, we have all been meditating on the weekends. So, why did Tanish and Aarav agree to my idea? Because of two arguments:

- 11 to 14 minutes of meditation will take up less than 1 per cent of their day.
- Rather than doing it every day, just two days a week of meditation was a comfortable start.

This little incident was insightful to me in more than one way. Not only did I harness the power of Small is

Big to convince my children to take up meditation, I also realized the inherent influencing power built into the idea of *small*. When you harness the power of small to convince a person to do or not do something, they are immediately more receptive to it. It makes them feel less intimidated by the magnitude of the task they are being asked to do and creates a secure feeling in them. Beautiful, isn't it, what 'Small is big' can help achieve in our lives?

Practice of Gratitude

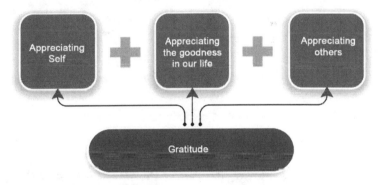

Fig. 3.5: The Three Levels of Gratitude

Appreciating Self

We tend to appreciate everyone and everything around us. How about appreciating ourselves? Yes, you read that right. It is essential to love yourself for the good qualities you think you have?

Thank you, Amit, for finding the time to meditate daily. It makes you more receptive, creative and calm. And it is when you are calm that you can help others.

For those who are not used to appreciating themselves, doing this may feel difficult and awkward. But it is an important task. Only when you understand yourself can you know others. An empty container cannot be used to serve water. Here are two simple ways in which you can get the process going:

- Identify a quality in yourself that you feel deserves appreciation. Close your eyes. Inhale and exhale slowly. Mindful breathing is key to this exercise.
- Express your thoughts verbally.

'Thank you <Your Name> or 'I am grateful to myself' for <the quality you wish to appreciate>. This has helped <you/others> to <the positive effect your quality has had on yourself /the larger community>.'

Alternatively, you can choose to perform this exercise by standing in front of a mirror. Face yourself with happiness and pride and repeat the above words.

Another great way to improve the effectiveness of this exercise is to incorporate gratitude in your meditation. As you meditate, appreciate the best qualities that you think you have.

Appreciating the Goodness in Our Life

One must appreciate all the beautiful things that life has given us. A straightforward way to do this is by maintaining a *gratitude journal*. Keeping a gratitude journal is a fulfilling and uplifting experience. When you write down everything you are grateful for, you'll begin to notice a positive change in your outlook. If you are having a bad day, your journal will remind you of everything you must be happy about. If you are having a good day, it will only multiply your happiness.

How you can go about this

A person experiences gratitude in five significant aspects of life: *Personal Life, Professional Life, Spiritual Wellness, Financial Wellness and Health.*

Find three things for each aspect that you are grateful for. Yes, there can be a million things that you will feel lucky you have. But, remember, 'Small is big'. Focusing on just three things will have a transformative effect.

I am deeply grateful for _____ *because it has* _____. *Thank you.*

For example:

I am deeply grateful for having a happy family because it gives me immense joy to come home to their smiling faces and unwavering support. Thank you.

I am deeply thankful for meeting my targets this year because it encourages me to achieve new goals. Thank you.

I am deeply grateful that I found the time to incorporate exercise into my daily routine because it keeps me focused and healthy. Thank you.

In this way, identify three things you are thankful for in every sphere of life. Then, attempt to make the gratitude journal a way of life . . . a daily habit. I know the next question. Daily habit? Do we have the time for it? Friends, this entire exercise will take only 5 to 7 minutes of the

1440 minutes you have in a day. That translates into 0.34 per cent to 0.48 per cent of your daily time. See the power of 'Small is big' as the source code for transformation. Just 5–7 minutes of your day can be extremely effective in helping you achieve mindfulness and contentment.

Appreciating Others

To complete the experience of gratitude, you must appreciate others who contribute to making your life happier and positive.

Remember when a dear friend or family member appreciated your contribution in improving some aspect of their lives? Remember the time your colleagues or seniors admired your work? The second you think about those moments, you begin to feel uplifted and happy. This is precisely what someone else feels when you appreciate them. Saying a simple 'thank you' or expressing admiration for what someone has done or achieved may seem small gestures, but they have a profound impact. It immediately enhances your bonding with the individual.

The next time you sit down with your gratitude journal, appreciate someone who has made you feel good or has positively impacted your thoughts.

Thank you <name of the person> for <what he/she has done for you>. This has helped me in <the change it has brought in your life>. This has helped others by <how it has directly or indirectly impacted those around you>.

For example:
Thank you, Mother, for teaching me to be kind and hard-working. Such values have helped me achieve my goals,

personally and professionally. It makes me a better parent, partner and son.

It is important to remember that there is no hard and fast moment or any particular time in the day when you can express your gratitude or write down your thoughts. Be grateful for the little things every moment of your life—the water you drink; the food you eat; the happy conversations you have with your loved ones. They deserve your appreciation. I call these instances *gratitude moments*. It is about seizing the moment you are in to express your gratitude to someone. As you read this book, stop for a second. Close your eyes, think about a positive experience and thank the Universe for giving it to you.

Self-talk

Finally, we reach the third activity that encourages sound mental health: self-talk.

Self-talk is a profound concept for improving one's mental health. It is how you talk to yourself. These are the thoughts you have in your head and heart . . . about yourself as a person. Some may even call it their *inner voice*. Have you noticed how you talk to yourself about the person that you are? Is it empowering or disempowering?

Examples of empowering self-talk would be:
- *I serve my community with truth and dedication, and I will continue to do so.*
- *I believe in sharing insights that my clients find valuable.*
- *I give my best in every small or big task.*
- *Working in start-ups helps me contribute in the growth of country's economy.*

- *Doing daily meditation is like giving food to my mind. When my mind gets food, it provides nourishment to all body parts.*

Disempowering or negative self-talk will be:
- *My team is very uncooperative. I always land up with uncooperative teams.*
- *Why don't I have enough money? Perhaps this is my fate.*
- *Why are my parents never pleased with my achievements? I feel bad when they glorify my sister's achievements.*
- *I am always tired. There is no way out.*
- *I lack confidence as a speaker. I will surely fumble every time I speak in front of people.*

In the above examples, the person reduces himself or herself to being a victim of circumstances.

Self-talk is all about sowing the seeds of intention.

When we empower ourselves through encouraging self-talk, we sow seeds of positivity.

When we victimize ourselves through discouraging self-talk, we sow seeds of negativity.

This precisely reflects the impact of thoughts on our well-being, as we discussed earlier. The nature of your thoughts and self-talk has a bearing on how you lead your life and make your decisions.

So, the ball is in your court. The next time you think about yourself, ask your mind, 'Which seed am I sowing? How do I sow the seeds of positivity so that the universe can respond accordingly?'

When repeated, inspiring self-talk becomes a habit—where you affirm good feelings and positive 'vibes' . . . about YOURSELF!

An easy exercise will help you get started on this:

1. Write three negative self-talk statements that you use
    frequently.

    _____

    _____

    _____

2. Once done, reflect on the following:

    *   *What are the negative repercussions of each of my
        statements?*

    *   *When I stop using them, what possibilities may
        open for me?*

3. With a firm intention to stop negative self-talk, strike
    out each of the three statements. The physical act
    of striking them out will create a lasting impact on
    your mind and reinforce your intentions to stop your
    negative self-talk.

4. Now, write three positive self-talk statements that you
    use or would like to use.

    _____

    _____

    _____

Writing and Repetition act as force multipliers. Writing
increases the intensity of a positive self-talk statement.
Daily Repetition makes it a habit.

Learning Accelerator

It is your turn to reflect upon the five pillars of your life. Write down your thoughts and think about a valuable micro-habit you can start and/or stop to improve your well-being in each of the areas.

Area	Problem	Start	Stop
Work			
Family			
Personal Finance			
Physical Health			
Mental Health			

4

The Law of Resonance:
One Catalyst for Holistic Change

*'If you want to find the secrets of the universe,
think in terms of energy, frequency and vibration.'*

—Nikola Tesla, Serbian-American
inventor and futurist

Resonance

Remember this word from physics class? Let's quickly jog
our memory.

*When two objects possess identical natural frequencies,
vibrations in one item will trigger vibrations in the other. This
phenomenon is called resonance.*

The most common way of demonstrating resonance
is by studying the behaviour of pendulums. Along
these lines, an excellent experiment was carried out by

The Physics Classroom.[6] The researcher set up a unique apparatus. It consisted of two groups of pendulums, each group containing three. One group mirrored the other. So, each pendulum had an identical twin. A pendulum and its twin were of the same length and vibrational frequency. It was noticed that when one pendulum was set into motion, its twin began to vibrate along with it.

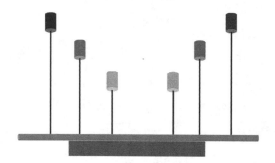

Fig. 4.1: Pendulum Apparatus

What is interesting is that vibrations are triggered in only identical pendulums. This is important for us to know. Why is that so? I'll get to discussing that.

Albert Einstein said, 'Everything in life is vibration.' All matter is made of atoms built of electrons, protons and neutrons that vibrate at specific regularity. As an extension of Einstein's statement, we as human beings too must vibrate at particular frequencies. Using this belief, can the Law of Resonance be applied in our lives?

In 2016, I attended a workshop conducted by Universe/City Mikael (UCM). They are a non-profit

---

[6] 'Resonance', The Physics Classroom, 30 January 2011, https://www.youtube.com/watch?v=tnS0SYF4pYE.

teaching and research centre specializing in emotional intelligence, symbolic language, meditation, yoga and dreams-signs-symbols interpretation. In this UCM workshop, I was first introduced to the Law of Resonance. The workshop began with a fantastic video[7] showing a construction worker helping a little boy who has had a fall on the road. The child thanks the man. Later, the same boy sees an older woman struggling to carry her bags. He steps in and helps carry her groceries across the street. In this way, the cycle of help continues. The video's purpose was to highlight *how a chain reaction was created because everyone resonated with the frequency of goodness.*

In simple words, the Law of Resonance means that *whatever is happening in our lives is governed by a small but compelling percentage of our innermost self.* This percentage attracts us to different situations. Precisely like a pendulum, we each resonate at a specific frequency, which causes certain kinds of benefits and problems. Think of this concept as an advanced and more philosophical version of the 'like attracts like' philosophy. If something unpleasant is happening, we resonate negatively. If something happy is happening, we resonate positively. Let's see examples of the different kinds of resonance and what they mean.

Negative resonance

- You are an optimistic person yet continually encounter situations where people are pessimistic and always challenging you.

---

[7] LifeVestInside, 'Life Vest Inside—Kindness Boomerang—"One Day"', 30 August 2011, https://www.youtube.com/watch?v=nwAYpLVyeFU.

There is a small percentage within you that remains pessimistic and challenges people or your own self.

- You are a go-getter, but the people around you are always delaying tasks and therefore your work.

There is a small percentage within you that is lazy and content with the delay.

- Irrespective of where you work, you've always had aggressive superiors.

There is a small percentage within you that has or continues to use authority negatively. You may be using authority negatively in any form as a manager, as a parent, as a sibling.

- You want your house to be neat and tidy and hold your family members responsible whenever you find the house dirty.

There is a small percentage within you that is lethargic and is fine with the house being untidy.

Positive resonance

- When you meet strangers from any walk of life, you instantly build a rapport with them.

There is a small percentage within you that loves to socialize and enjoys camaraderie.

- You enjoy material success and, at the same time, are curious about meditation and spiritual health.

There is a small percentage within you that likes the balance of spiritual and material aspects.

- You think big. Simultaneously, you celebrate the smaller things in life.

There is a small percentage within you that is a visionary, someone who understands that big things are built by small things.

The critical point of the Law of Resonance lies in *acknowledging* and *taking responsibility* for that small percentage within ourselves that is the root cause of the different happenings in our life. Rather than attribute these happenings to your external surroundings, the law upholds the importance of self-acknowledgement and accountability. Perhaps because of this reason, the Law of Resonance is the most important law for personal and spiritual development. When Ananda, Lord Buddha's disciple, asked him, 'What will we do when you or any other master is not present on Earth to show us the path of truth?' the Buddha answered, *'Apo Dipo Bhava*. Be your own light.'* Here, Light symbolizes the source of holistic growth. The Buddha taught us to take responsibility for our own personal growth and not shift our burden to others.

Similarly, the Law of Resonance empowers us to see the light within ourselves by allowing us to evaluate and change our frequency. As we work on enhancing the intensity of our inner light, darkness is removed. We illuminate our souls and minds and, in turn, inspire others whom we encounter.

Think about this. If we focus on unlocking the light within us, imagine the collective illumination that 7.7 billion people can create.

Ever since I understood the impact of the Law of Resonance, I started accepting every negative situation in my life and always attempted to look within to find solutions to them. Acknowledging a challenge and focusing on your inner self to overcome it are the two pillars of the Law of Resonance. When you begin to follow the two pillars, the toxic blame game or victim mindset withers away.

Let me give an example of Law of Resonance and its magical impact on my professional life.

In 2017, I was heading the revenue function for an organization. We were on a growth trajectory and our clients were pleased with our products and service. However, the client was not paying us according to the payment schedule. Indeed, it was unusual behaviour on their part and a big problem for a start-up like ours. It was bizarre, and I kept thinking to myself, 'Why are the clients not paying on time even though they are happy with our work?'

It was then that I remembered the Law of Resonance. I thought to myself, 'As the head of revenue, do I have a resonant frequency within me that is causing such a situation? Do I have pending payments to make?'

As I reflected on this, I first acknowledged the problem and then immediately started making any payments that were due or were delayed. In some cases, I started paying well in advance. The change that followed was almost unbelievable. That quarter, we had the highest recorded collections! Acknowledgement and action helped me change my resonant frequency to a higher level and a higher resonant frequency enabled a new reality. All that happened because I applied the Law of Resonance.

As you can see, the Law of Resonance is exceptionally impactful in helping us alter our reality. It is a step-by-step process:

Step 1: *Acknowledge* the small percentage within you as the cause of negative situations in your life and *desire to work on yourself.*

Step 2: *Take action.* This action can be taken in four steps:

- **Changing our thoughts**
  When trying to solve the payment issue with my clients, I decided to stop being disturbed and emerge from that unresourceful state. I changed my thoughts and adopted a solution-oriented, resourceful approach.
- **Conscious physical action**
  Reflective thoughts are the first step to success. However, the reflections must be transformed into concrete actions. I cleared all my dues and made advance payments. That was a decisive action on my part.
- **Changing our habits**
  In the previous chapter, we extensively discussed habits and addictions, and also how to adopt effective

micro-habits for enhancing our wellness in the five pillars of our life.

- **Mindfulness**
Mindfulness is the key to enhancing emotional intelligence and achieving mental wellness. As discussed in the previous chapter, it is the state of being equanimous, calm and composed in positive or negative situations. *Meditation*, *Practice of Gratitude* and *Self-talk* are the techniques one can follow to change one's frequencies for the better.

Imagine what will happen if we understand, acknowledge and implement this extraordinary principle of self-development and actualization called the Law of Resonance. It has the potential to inspire the most significant transformations in our lives.

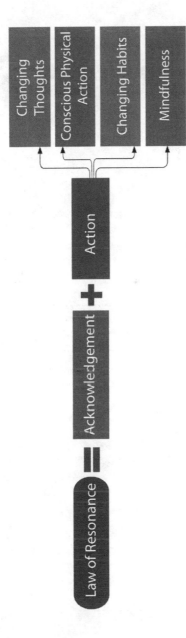

Fig. 4.2: The Law of Resonance: How to Change your Reality

Learning Accelerator

1. Identify three positive resonances and their impact on
   your life.

   Positive resonance 1:

   _____

   Impact:

   _____

   Positive resonance 2:

   _____

   Impact:

   _____

   Positive resonance 3:

   _____

   Impact:

   _____

2. Identify three negative resonances and their impact
   on your life.

   Negative resonance 1:

   _____

   Impact:

   _____

Negative resonance 2:

_____

Impact:

_____

Negative resonance 3:

_____

Impact:

_____

3. For each negative resonance, please identify:
   Acknowledgement: Is there a small percentage in me causing this negative resonance?
   Action: What are the powerful ways in which I can change this?

   • Thoughts:

   _____

   • Physical actions:

   _____

   • Habits:

   _____

   • Mindfulness:

   _____

Summary of 'Small is Big': Transforming Life

To achieve a big transformation in our lives, we need to focus our energies on only three small areas.

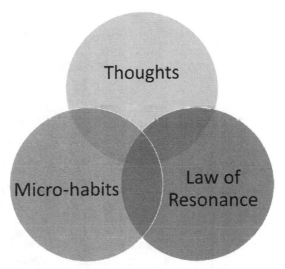

PART II

'Small Is Big'
Transforming Business

Introduction

I s business different from life?
Are there similarities between them? Are there differences between them?

Some of you will say, 'The way we act in business is different from the way we act in life.'

Some of you will say, 'Business is a part of life.'

For me, life is the superset, and business a subset of it.

Therefore, the thoughts, micro-habits and resonances we have in life impact our approach towards business too. They determine our attitude and, by logical extension, the challenges and successes we face in our professional life.

How does that happen? Let's see.

Thoughts

Two organizations are coming together for a merger. As an employee, there are two ways one can perceive the event.

Positive thought: It will be interesting to see what changes will happen in my role because of this merger.

I hope I get to learn something new. If I don't, there are always other opportunities outside.

Negative thought: Oh my goodness! This will be such a pain. Maybe this means a new boss and a new team, and God knows what their attitude will be like. I don't want any change in my role.

A single thought triggers an associated positive or negative chain reaction. It not only impacts the very moment in which you are living but also affects your entire workday, month and so on.

By reframing the situation, expressing gratitude and harnessing resourceful memories, a negative outlook can be refurbished into a positive one.

Micro-Habits

Let's look at few examples

Rather than coming to office by 9 a.m., most corporate leaders arrive between 11 a.m. and noon. Their subordinates follow the same pattern. Nobody realizes that this has become an ingrained habit.

A sales owner is accustomed to meeting customers in person. But due to the pandemic, he is not able to meet them face to face. In a one-to-one call, his boss asks him: 'How are you?' The sales owner replies, 'I feel that I don't have a job because I cannot meet my customers.' Physical in-person interactions have become a habit. Any change in them, like virtual selling, may result in insecurity and resistance for a traditional sales owner.

Resonance

An execution-focused executive successively finds himself in company environments where employees agree to do something but don't execute it. He is surprised and angry. Maybe this is the time for him to look deeper into his resonance. Is there a small part within him that hinders execution in real life? Acknowledging his contribution to the situation and changing it will create a chain reaction in the external surroundings and improve the work environment.

We have seen how 'Small is big' was incorporated by people in business for their own improvement by implementing the previous section's principles on transforming life. However, can we expand the application of 'Small is big' to cover several other aspects of business comprehensively?

Yes, we can. And interestingly, in more ways than one!

The next part of the book goes more in-depth, exploring practical ways in which 'Small is big' can be implemented in both the strategic and tactical elements of a business. We will explore the following six areas where business can be transformed by executing small changes.

Organizational Culture: Micro-changes for Macro-effect
Small Wins, Small Goals: Unlocking Big Milestones
Avoiding a Crowd: Strength in Small Teams

Keep it Short: The Power of Small Meetings
Choosing Your Niche: Fewer Products, Fewer Problems
Concise and Captivating: Five Pointers for Crisp
Business Presentations

Let us begin our journey and see how 'Small is big' can fuel growth in business.

5

Organizational Culture: Micro-Changes for Macro-Effect

'The stronger the culture, the less corporate
process a company needs.
When the culture is strong, you can trust
everyone to do the right thing.'

—Brian Chesky, co-founder and
CEO, Airbnb

If we imagine an organization as a healthy tree, then the organizational culture lies in its roots. The roots of a tree are invisible to the human eye. They grow underground, yet roots are what keeps the tree in place and nourishes it. Organizational culture may not be a tangible entity, but it defines the strength and health of the work environment. While it may seem like an abstract concept, culture is seen and felt in many ways: in how employees handle tasks, in how teams are made, in how challenges are addressed, successes acknowledged and, finally, in what factors motivate or discourage progress. In short, culture encompasses *what* work is being done, *how* it is being done and *why* it is being done.

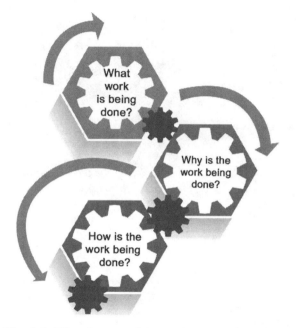

Fig. 5.1: The Gears of Organizational Culture

Let's observe the following real-life scenarios to understand this better.

Scenario 1: Organization A has a salesforce of fifteen people, a mere 2 per cent of its 700 employees. The company does not have a routine for timely payment of incentives to this force. A sales owner has to repeatedly ask for the incentives rather than have them paid to him or her automatically and according to a fixed schedule. The members of the sales team feel tired and frustrated.

The company culture: One of informal processes and lack of structure.

The company risks: Sales attrition and low revenues.

Scenario 2: Organization B has 450 employees. Darren joins the company after working for a much larger organization. Here he finds a strange phenomenon within just two weeks of joining. The majority of the people asked to attend a meeting do not accept the invite yet casually join in the discussion. Sometimes Darren receives a declined request, but with no reason or explanation provided. He is perplexed and finds this rude. Within only two weeks of his joining, he feels disconnected with the company.

The company culture: Lack of mutual respect and decorum.

The company risks: Disconnected teams and an absence of warmth and empathy.

Scenario 3: Organization C has many employees, most of them with a tenure of five to ten years. Many joined when the organization was in its infancy and are very close to the founder. As the company has grown, new leaders have been inducted into the organization. Even though some of the older employees report to the new leaders, they tend to break protocol and keep reaching out to the founder. Sometimes, this leads to an unnecessary escalation in almost trivial matters.

The company culture: A hail-the-founder attitude and a tendency to constantly please people.

The company risks: Serious scalability challenges and attrition of new leaders.

Each of the cases is true to life. Each of their small failings poses significant risks for the companies. Together, they can create the cumulative effect of almost derailing an organization from its growth path. Rather than adopt a big bang approach aiming for massive cultural change, organizations and leaders need to observe and address the smaller, more minute phenomena in their companies occurring at the ground level. By bringing about a positive difference in how departments and teams function at the micro-level, one can trigger a macro-effect. Imagine if Organization A began to release incentives on time, Organization B tried to create a culture of respect and responsiveness, and a new employee in Organization C challenged its hail-the-founder attitude and received support from the leadership. Minuscule steps, aren't they? But it's the scale of their impact that will make us experience the worth of small changes. They contain the power to beautifully transform the organizational ethos and enhance the quality of the work environment. This will change the organization into an institution brimming with warmth, support and opportunities for growth.

Learning Accelerator

As a part of a function, ask yourself the following question:
'If I had to address only three situations now that can foster a culture of camaraderie and growth in <function name>, which three would I list?'

Situation 1

_____

_____

_____

Situation 2

_____

_____

_____

Situation 3

_____

_____

_____

Once you are done listing them, prioritize them as Priority 1, Priority 2 and Priority 3.

Your next course of action is to reflect on how to bring about these *three* changes to encourage a healthier work atmosphere.

Start small. As few as three changes can make a big difference.

6

Small Wins, Small Goals: Unlocking Big Milestones

'Less is more. Progress is made through precise, persistent and purposeful pushes.'

—Scott Perry, author of *Endeavor: Thrive Through Work Aligned with Your Values, Talents, and Tribe*

When do organizations prosper? When they make inspiring progress in their field. And what is the primary driving force behind the creation and sustenance of progress?

Motivated employees, isn't it?

When employees are satisfied with their efforts and feel encouraged to achieve newer professional heights, an organization will enjoy phenomenal growth. In this journey of ensuring employee motivation, the 'Small is big' source code can make an everlasting impact. How is that going to happen?

In 2011, *Harvard Business Review*[8] published a comprehensive study on what keeps employees motivated to continue doing creative work. The study was conducted by means of a survey of 669 managers employed in companies across the world. The respondents were asked to rank the following managerial tools in order of their influence on employee work attitude:

• Support for the progress they have made in their work
• Recognition for good work
• Incentives
• Interpersonal support
• Clear goals

Further, to study the link between inner work-life balance and professional performance, the *Harvard Business Review* research team analysed 12,000 diary entries made by 238 individuals working across twenty-six project teams. An employee's inner work-life balance relates to their feelings, motivation and perception. An employee with a positive inner work-life balance will perform better than one with a poor work-life balance.

---

[8] T.M. Amabile and S.J. Kramer, 'The Power of Small Wins', *Harvard Business Review* (May 2011), https://hbr.org/2011/05/the-power-of-small-wins.

The two studies conducted with managers and employees revealed a startling difference in how each group perceived professional motivation.

Can you guess which managerial tool emerged as the most significant motivating factor for employees? The results revealed that most employees selected *support for their progress in work* as the chief influence that encourages them to do better. When employees feel a sense of progress, it inspires them to work energetically and creatively.

However, it was surprising that managers were in the dark about what fuels and boosts employee motivation. Most of the participating managers selected *recognition for good work* and *tangible incentives* as the driving force behind employees doing better work. Interestingly, only 5 per cent of managers ranked support for progress as the #1 stimulus. The study highlights the lacuna that exists in managerial understanding of the root source of employee motivation.

The findings of the study can be imagined as having the structure of an iceberg (see Fig. 6.1). Above the surface, we only see its comparatively smaller tip or *recognition for good work*. But below the water is the colossal portion that stays hidden. For us, that is *support for progress*. Although this is usually invisible, it is the more powerful of the two and needs greater attention.

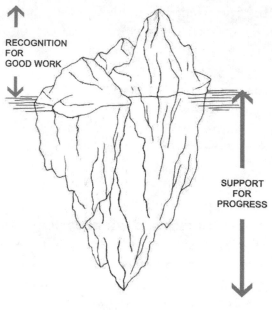

Fig. 6.1

The study revealed that ordinary and *incremental progress* could enhance people's engagement and happiness, leading to better inner work-life balance. Notably, 28 per cent of the incidents that had a minor effect on an ongoing project significantly impacted people's feelings about it. The authors concluded that small but consistent progress could result in remarkable execution.

As we reflect on concepts such as professional progress and motivation, the question that comes to my mind is: *What is the source of fulfilment?* Is it always the result of huge breakthroughs, or can we experience satisfaction by achieving consistent and incremental progress?

Let's try and apply the concept of incremental progress and small wins to a relatable business scenario.

In the world of sales, the most important milestone is the signed contract. However, the road to the signed contract has several smaller landmarks. These include getting a prospective meeting, creating a demo, submitting a quality proposal that impresses the clients, finding support for developing relevant case studies, and convincing clients to agree to another meeting to discuss the project and further negotiations. They are all vital for the closing the deal. Team leaders must identify and recognize such intermediate milestones and actively create a culture of focusing on and executing these smaller goals. Once the habit of achieving smaller goals and getting recognition for these is ingrained in the team, employees enjoy a sense of steady growth. As a manager, you must align the team effort towards incremental progress and create a supportive atmosphere that acknowledges small goals and accomplishments. Congratulate the team every step of the way. Sometimes, make time for a cup of coffee with the team to celebrate the completion of these essential *small* steps, without which the bigger picture cannot be achieved. It brings a sense of fulfilment and joy to the team. It uplifts and inspires everyone to do better. Moreover, leaders must realize that celebrating small wins doesn't need grand gestures. A *thank you* is a powerful way to recognize a milestone.

In December 2020, my team and I worked with a strategic Quick Service Restaurant (QSR) client in South-east Asia. The client was running losses because of the pandemic, and the deal was taking longer than usual. In between, we had a video call with the CEO, and he asked us to create a one-page business case for their perusal. We worked for more than a week to build that one-pager. Yes, can you imagine that just a one-page business case took more than seven days to make? Again, a testament to 'Small is big'—where a concise one-pager made the difference.

When I received the final version, I was delighted with it. I immediately wrote to my team and praised their excellent work. I called the sales and pre-sales owners and heartily appreciated the beautiful outcome. Throughout the conversation, I could sense warmth and positivity. While managers or group heads must recognize the minor milestones, it is more critical for employees to realize the virtue of small wins. It is an invaluable component of self-development.

Finally, the question that remains is: how does one build this culture of recognizing smaller milestones? There are three ways:

First and foremost, it is the manager's responsibility to commence this practice of concentrating on steady progress and small wins. By ensuring that this approach is repeated, leaders can successfully transform it into an admirable and positive habit among their team. When team heads acknowledge small achievements, it stimulates an environment where it becomes a way of life; a constructive tradition that hugely benefits the organizational spirit.

Secondly, as an employee at any level of the organization, you can cultivate a habit of acknowledgement by asking yourself a simple question at the end of each day: *'In which three areas did I make incremental progress today?'* The moment you find your answer, you'll realize that the little ways in which you made progress during the day contain the power to generate big waves of happiness. This practice will significantly improve professional growth as you will feel resourceful and satisfied.

Finally, managers and employees often have the intention to bring about positive change but require additional support and someone to point them in the right direction. Here, the role of human resources becomes essential. HR must consider scheduling appropriate training sessions on the importance of setting and executing small goals. When external trainers share best practices, it will fuel desire within the organization to celebrate minor milestones.

It is fascinating to observe how, beyond business research, spirituality and science have always spoken about the importance of implementing smaller goals.

Let's take the example of the Bhagavad Gita, a revered Hindu scripture considered to be a cornerstone of spiritual practice and literature. In this beautiful scripture, we come across two beautiful verses of invaluable wisdom about not worrying about the results of one's actions, which by implication means concentrating on the process.

Chapter II, Verse 47

कर्मण्येवाधिकारस्ते मा फलेषु कदाचन । मा कर्मफलहेतुर्भुर्मा ते संगोऽस्त्वकर्मणि

You have the right to perform your duties only, but you are never entitled to the result.

Don't be driven by results, nor be attached to inaction.

Chapter III: Verse 19

तस्मादसक्तः सततं कार्यं कर्म समाचर
असक्तो ह्याचरन्कर्म परमाप्नोति पूरुषः

Therefore, without being attached to the fruits of activities, one should act as a matter of duty; by working without attachment, one attains the Supreme.

In business, goals often fail because we become fixated on the outcome, or what the Gita terms as *being attached to the fruits of activities*. When efforts are only focused on that one big revenue goal or that upcoming massive product launch, it makes the team fearful and insecure. The verses remind us to be focused on our duties and actions rather than becoming feverish when we think about the outcome. In the practical world, the easiest way to achieve great results is to divide the journey into a set of smaller steps and take effective action to fulfil each goal. You still have goals (results) here to think about, but since they are small, they don't weigh you down so heavily. This may sound like a straightforward approach, but many organizations find it challenging to implement. The next time you plan for a great outcome in the organization, remember the golden verses mentioned above. They fuel an action-oriented mindset while detaching one's thoughts from the outcome.

In chemistry and physics, we find ample evidence of science bestowing importance to small goals and wins. Dopamine ($C_8H_{11}NO_2$) is a chemical released by the brain when we feel a sense of reward or pleasure. When we accomplish small goals, we experience satisfaction because of the release of this chemical. For this reason, dopamine is often called the reward or pleasure molecule. This is why participants in the *Harvard Business Review* study felt happy and resourceful when they made incremental progress. As humans, we are chemically designed to set small goals and derive a sense of achievement upon their completion.

Recall the domino effect phenomenon we discussed in the chapter on habits. We observed how a gentle push to the smallest domino has the potential to topple the largest one. The fall of each domino represents the completion of a small goal. Each fall of the domino generates *kinetic energy* substantial enough to topple the next one. This creates a chain reaction of energy, with the energy produced in the end emerging as nearly 2 billion times more potent than that of the first gentle tap.

In conclusion, I wish to present a practical framework that will help teams to inculcate a culture of small wins. The structure is founded on three Ss: *Small, Specific* and *Smile*.

Small: Divide big goals into small steps.

Specific: Get clarity on date and ownership.

Smile: Celebrate with a smile, the completion of small and specific goals.

SMILE: Smile is about celebrating the completion of small and specific goals.

SPECIFIC: Specific refers to clarity on date and ownership.

SMALL: Divide big goals into small milestones.

Fig. 6.2: The 3 S Framework for Setting and Executing Small Goals

When you complete a small, specific goal with the organization's support, your satisfaction, in the form of a smile, will be an automated response due to dopamine release. In turn, you too can enjoy the completion of small goals with your colleagues with a small celebration, thereby triggering a beautiful and warm smile among your team.

Business operations progress towards a long-term goal. And while the joy of achieving a significant target is a beautiful feeling, it is even more critical that companies, managers and employees begin to accord importance to the smaller victories that happen along the way. Executing micro-goals and acknowledging small successes foster an atmosphere of bonding, positivity and motivation. They inspire respect for the journey and for the progress of events and do not engender a blind commitment to the destination. Set *small* goals, celebrate the completion of *small* wins and watch the team achieve *big* landmarks.

Learning Accelerator

1. In your current work environment, closely observe how the following managerial tools fare when it comes to employee motivation and tick in the appropriate boxes.

Tool	High	Medium	Low
Support for the progress employees have made in their work			
Recognition for good work			
Incentives			
Interpersonal support			
Clear goals			

2. Think of three steps that can cultivate the small-wins mindset in you.

_____

_____

_____

3. Think of three steps that can cultivate the small-wins
    mindset among your team.

    _____

    _____

    _____

4. List the top *three* business goals you plan to achieve in
    the next twelve months. Divide the goal into smaller
    milestones.

    Goal 1: _____

S. No.	Milestones	Estimated Date of Completion
1.		
2.		
3.		

    Goal 2: _____

S. No.	Milestones	Estimated Date of Completion
1.		
2.		
3.		

Goal 3: _____

S. No.	Milestones	Estimated Date of Completion
1.		
2.		
3.		

7

Avoiding a Crowd: Strength in Small Teams

'If you can't feed a team with two pizzas, it's too large.'

—Jeff Bezos, founder and CEO,
Amazon

Jeff Bezos's words are simple, yet so powerful in highlighting the power of small teams. Many of the tasks in our professional lives revolve around brainstorming with our colleagues, and excellent teamwork is central to the achievement of targets. But how does the size of the team impact its work? What is the ideal number of people in a group, exceeding which it becomes challenging for the group to coordinate and create something new and exciting?

To explore the impact of team size, researchers Dashun Wang, James A. Evans and Lingfei Wu analysed over 65 million papers, patents and software products released between 1954 and 2014.[9] The results of their studies were quite fascinating. The study noticed a nearly universal pattern in how large teams and their smaller counterparts worked. Large teams were likely to develop and further existing designs and ideas. On the other hand, smaller groups tended to disrupt current thinking methods with innovative ideas and opportunities.

Simply put, large teams excel at solving problems. And small groups are likely to think of new challenges for their sizeable counterparts to solve. Large units are expected to build on recent, popular ideas, while small teams reach further into the past or look into the future and source inspiration from seemingly obscure ideas and possibilities. The research compared large groups to large movie studios which are more likely to produce sequels than create something new. According to the authors, *'We found that as team size grows from 1 to 50 members, the associated level of disruption drops precipitously.'*

Interestingly, this wasn't the first time that people had examined the challenges encountered by large working teams. Around a century ago, the French agricultural engineer Maximilien Ringelmann (1861–1931) coined the term 'Ringelmann Effect'. This is a phenomenon in which individual members of a group exhibit declining productivity as the group's size increases. Ringelmann corroborated his findings using the tug-of-war game as

---

[9] D. Wang and J.A. Evans, 'Research: When Small Teams Are Better than Big Ones', *Harvard Business Review*, 21 February 2019, https://hbr.org/2019/02/research-when-small-teams-are-better-than-big-ones.

an example. The more people that pulled a rope, the less effort each person contributed. Ringelmann believed that as more and more participants become involved, each individual begins to feel that their action is not critical for the endeavour's success. This is the result of a loss of motivation and coordination in large settings.

Jennifer Mueller, a Wharton management professor, identified another determinative influence on the individual's behaviour in large groups. In her research,[10] 'Why Individuals in Larger Teams Perform Worse', Mueller studied 212 knowledge workers from twenty-six teams, ranging from three to nineteen members in size. Alongside a decline in motivation and coordination, she found a third form of loss, called 'Relational Loss', which causes a significant decline in a person's performance in a big team. It is defined as a type of individual-level process loss, wherein an employee thinks that support, help and assistance are less available when the number of members in the team increases. This loss encompasses perceptions about the degree to which teammates are likely to provide assistance and support when the individual is faced with struggle.

Relational loss can happen because of a further lack of four types of support:

1. Emotional support: the expression of trust and positive emotions towards teammates when they are faced with struggle

---

[10] J. S. Mueller, 'Why Individuals in Larger Teams Perform Worse', Organizational Behavior and Human Decision Processes, *Science Direct*, 117(1), pp. 111–124, January 2012, https://doi.org/10.1016/j.obhdp.2011.08.004.

2. Instrumental support: help and assistance from teammates
3. Appraisal support: advice to help teammates overcome setbacks
4. Informational support: sharing of knowledge, to help members solve problems

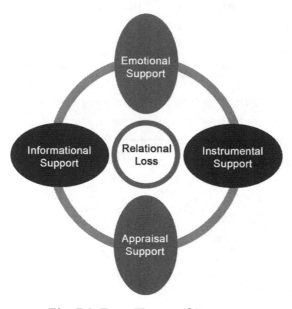

Fig. 7.1: Four Types of Support

Both[11] Ringelmann and Mueller assert the impact team size has on an individual's performance. So, the question arises as to what is the optimal team size for fuelling performance.

---

[11] 'Is Your Team Too Big? Too Small? What's the Right Number?' Knowledge@ Wharton, The Wharton School, University of Pennsylvania, 14 June 2006, https://knowledge.wharton.upenn.edu/article/is-your-team-too-big-too-small-whats-the-right-number-2/

Channelling Ringelmann's theories in her paper, Mueller concluded that it depends on the task at hand. For example, if the job is to clean a stadium, the more the number of janitors the faster the work is done. There is no limit to the size of that team. But when companies are dealing with coordination and motivational issues and are trying to build the optimal team, it immediately correlates to a six-member group. More than five, one begins to notice diminishing motivation. Post the fifth member, Mueller finds that people start to look for cliques.

In my professional life, I have experienced the strength of smaller teams.

From November 2020, rather than giving tasks to a large team, I began allocating work to teams of two or three individuals.

For example, I would ask one person to create a pricing sheet and get it reviewed by one other team member.

Another team member would need to create a template for the CEO's monthly review and then seek his colleagues' inputs.

Two others would have to finalize the criteria for getting 150K ARR (Annual Recurring Revenue) accounts for a specific product.

The new approach yielded excellent results! Each task was getting done and exceeding my expectations, both in terms of time and quality. As I reflected on this, I realized that this notable change happened because of two reasons: smaller team and smaller scope. When you consolidate the team and reduce the number of participants, you create an open space that encourages accountability, hands-on involvement and healthy collaboration.

Learning Accelerator

In your current organizational/team structure, identify three areas where you can create smaller teams. While significant structural changes in the organization may take time, add areas where the 'Small is big' source code can be implemented at the earliest.

1. _____

2. _____

3. _____

8

Keeping it Short: The Power
of Small Meetings

'The longer the meeting, the less is accomplished.'

—Tim Cook, chief executive officer,
Apple Inc.

In the business context, why do we need meetings? What purpose do they serve? Meetings are an integral part of information sharing, brainstorming and reviewing progress. In our professional lives we have many meetings on a routine basis. But, while we are busy attending these meetings, have we ever wondered if we are conducting them efficiently?

In 2019, a study was conducted by Doodle,[12] the world's largest scheduling platform. The researchers studied 6500 professionals in the UK, US and Germany and examined 19 million meetings arranged on the platform in the previous year. The results of the study were startling. Doodle discovered the following trends:

- On an average, professionals spend three hours a week in meetings—making two-thirds of all meetings unnecessary or a waste of time.
- They spend two hours a week in meetings they find pointless. Taken collectively, it amounted to a waste of more than $541 billion in employee time in 2019.
- The average meeting is about an hour long. When meeting hours were combined, 24.75 billion hours were lost due to poorly organized meetings in 2019.

So, how can we utilize the 'Small is big' source code for efficient meetings? Let's begin by observing the three essential constituents of any meeting:

- Agenda (scope of the meeting)
- Duration
- Number of participants

---

[12] Doodle, 'The State of Meetings Report 2019', https://assets.ctfassets.net/ 8t3gydnqcry0/3TLe93eDXOK9jWQ9FpCysE/b660cc2e3f921f601 ddc5645548f5472/E-book_-_Meeting_Report_2019.pdf; https://doodle.com/ en/resources/research-and-reports-/the-state-of-meetings-2019/.

Agenda

'The secret of a successful and time-efficient meeting is preparation. The agenda mustn't be too long. Otherwise there's a risk of spending too much time on the first items and later items are rushed.'

—Dr Sankalp Chaturvedi, associate professor of organizational behaviour and leadership, Imperial College, London Business School

The first thing that meeting organizers must ascertain is: *What is the scope of the meeting?* Is the agenda addressing a particular concern, or is it too ambiguous and open-ended?

Allow me to share a real-life experience. In the past, I used to conduct sales reviews for all regions and products. Since our meetings' scope was more extensive, it would require more than ten people to join and lead discussions that exceeded an hour. Sometimes, speakers did not even get the chance to properly address the audience and were forced to wrap up their portion in a hurry.

In 2020, I changed the scope of such meetings from all products to one specific product line or segment. And although each call was set up for 45 minutes, I noticed that the review meetings successfully addressed all the areas in just 25–30 minutes. Moreover, each region received a chance to speak. The discussions were sharper. This resulted in a rather pleasant feeling of contentment and productivity among the team, especially when these meetings started happening regularly.

Big scope Higher probability of inefficient meetings	Small scope Higher probability of efficient meetings
One review meeting for all regions	Review meeting for a specific region
Review roadmap for all products	Review roadmap for a specific product
Review of all GTM (go-to-market) functions for a region	Separate reviews of sales, pre-sales, customer success, marketing and demand generation

Duration

'Work expands to fill the time available for its completion.'
—Parkinson's Law

How often have you felt bored, tired and agitated during those never-ending office meetings? In addition to a concentrated scope, meetings need to be short too. A mindset of '30 minutes or less' is required to conduct efficient meetings.

Marissa Mayer, former president and CEO of Yahoo, used to schedule 10-minute micro meetings.[13] While

---

[13] Steven Rogelberg, 'How to Reap Big Returns from Meetings That Are Just 10 to 15 Minutes Long,' *ideas.ted.com*, 5 September 2019, https://ideas.ted.com/how-to-reap-big-benefits-from-meetings-that-are-just-10-to-15-minutes-long/; David Fallarme, 'Run Your Meeting like a Boss: Lessons from Mayer, Musk, and Jobs', *99u*, 16 April 2014, https://99u.adobe.com/articles/25075/run-your-meeting-like-a-boss-lessons-from-mayer-musk-and-jobs; *Gamelearn* Team, 'How to run a meeting like Marissa Meyer (Yahoo)' *gamelearn*, https://www.game-learn.com/en/resources/blog/how-to-run-a-meeting-like-marissa-mayer-yahoo/

the number of sessions increased to seventy per week, it allowed her to respond to her employees' needs and get the team to create tighter agendas.

Percolate,[14] a leading content marketing platform, believes in the power of 15-minute meetings. They value this culture so highly that they framed six rules to ensure only productive, shorter sessions. Before a meeting is finalized, the team head is supposed to remember the following tenets:

- Do you really need a meeting?
- Meetings should be 15 minutes by default
- No spectators
- Have a purpose; state it up front
- Make tasks, assign them to people
- Don't bring computers or phones

Some organizations have even resorted to adopting formal means to ensure that meetings end on time. O3 World, a digital product agency, built a bot that reminds people to move out of meeting rooms when the time is up. Called Roombot,[15] the technology uses the Google Calendar API and Hue API to remind participants about the end time. It achieves this by dimming the lights in the room and sending an audio message. Compelling, isn't it?

In Tripping.com,[16] the leader contributes to the team's beer jar if the meeting does not end on time. In

---

[14] N. Brier, 'The 6 Meeting Rules of Percolate', *Percolate*, 9 June 2014, https://twitter.com/percolate/status/476033033330368515.

[15] 'Roombot: Solving Meetings One Room at a Time', *O3*, https://www.o3world.com/labs/roombot/

[16] Steven Rogelberg, 'How to Reap Big Returns from Meetings That Are Just 10 to 15 Minutes Long,' *ideas.ted.com*, 5 September 2019, https://ideas.ted.com/how-to-reap-big-benefits-from-meetings-that-are-just-10-to-15-minutes-long/

Buddytruk, if the session exceeds the time limit, the last speaker has to do fifty push-ups!

Inspired by the success of organizations that have made a conscious effort to schedule short discussions to address specific concerns, I decided to set up only 30-minute-long meetings. For even more exact agendas, I try to keep them under 15 minutes. For example, before discussing the criteria for $150,000 ARR accounts in Asia for advanced retail analytics, my team had already shared the content with me. That enabled me to have questions prepared beforehand. We were able to wrap up the discussion in less than 15 minutes, testifying that a specific plan and prior preparation go a long way in ensuring productive meetings.

Number of Participants

How often have you attended a meeting with more than ten people? And how often have you not got to express your thoughts because there were just too many attendees? So many times, a meeting becomes unmanageable because there are too many people. This also creates a lot of pressure on the attendees, with boredom, distress and loss of productivity creeping in.

Before we think of addressing this situation, have you wondered why we include a lot of people in a meeting? There can be three plausible causes:

- To cover an extensive agenda
- To satisfy a person's ego
- To prevent a backlash that may arise if someone is excluded

A simple question to ask yourself while arranging a meeting is: *'If I don't invite this person, will he/she and other team members miss out on something significant?'* The question acts as a practical *qualitative* filtering criterion.

You may also approach the situation *quantitatively,* where Miller's Law[17] comes to our rescue. Postulated by Harvard University Professor George A. Miller, the principle states that a human can hold 7 ± 2 objects in their short-term memory at one time. It is a beneficial technique to ensure optimum productivity. So, the next time a meeting is being set up, remember the magical number of seven for the meeting size.

Many meetings focus on the agenda at hand, and that's a good thing. But the real problem lies in the lack of clarity, both in the agenda and in the preparation for it. This three-point meeting template will help you address this roadblock and improve the quality of your meetings.

Meeting Template

Inputs and prerequisites: This includes material that you want the audience to read and any specific task that must be completed before the meeting.

Agenda: The specific concerns/issues/items that need to be discussed in the meeting,

Outcome: What would be the key outcomes of this meeting?

---

[17] 'The Magical Number Seven, Plus or Minus Two', https://en.wikipedia.org/wiki/The_Magical_Number_Seven,_Plus_or_Minus_Two

Inputs and Prerequisites
1.
2.
3.

Agenda
1.
2.
3.

Outcomes
1.
2.
3.

Wondering why only three points under each section? That's because, for optimal scope, you need not have more than three issues per meeting. If you aren't able to restrict your discussion to three points or less, it means that you need to schedule another meeting.

I have used this template for meetings that I have organized, and the benefits have been incredible. A planned template of this kind enables the following scenarios:

1. It shows that the person who has called for the meeting has clarity of thought and purpose. In turn, this may create two very different kinds of feelings among those attending: respect and irritation. A particular section may feel irritated because they are accustomed

to the old ways of receiving empty and vague meeting invites. But, rest assured, they will respect the initiative and the person who has organized it for going the extra mile to ensure a productive meeting.

2. A ready-made template brings both structure and brevity to the discussions.

3. The Inputs and Prerequisites and Outcome sections make every stakeholder accountable. It becomes every participant's responsibility to ensure that the discussion is fruitful and yields positive results.

The key to a successful meeting lies in aligning the three factors determining its success: agenda, duration and number of participants. When each of these dimensions is capped at the optimum level, the meeting will be more productive. Small meetings, significant results . . . that is the core philosophy!

Learning Accelerator

1. Select three factors that enable you to harness the power of 'Small is big' for efficient meetings.
   - ☐ A spacious and well-decorated meeting room
   - ☐ A specific agenda with less than three items
   - ☐ A meeting with more than ten outcomes
   - ☐ A meeting with seven or fewer than seven attendees
   - ☐ A meeting whose duration is less than 30 minutes

2. List three meeting scenarios where you can implement the three tenets of small meetings.

S. No.	Specific Agenda	Duration (</=30 mins)	Attendees Count (</=7)
1.			
2.			
3.			

3. For each of the above meeting scenarios, send your next meeting invite using the Three-Point Template.

9

Choosing Your Niche:
Fewer Products, Fewer Problems

'A designer knows he has achieved perfection
not when there is nothing more to add, but
when there is nothing left to take away.'

— Antoine de Saint-Exupéry,
French writer and poet

In 1996, Steve Jobs rejoined Apple as the organization's CEO. At that time, Apple was in a precarious position, on the verge of bankruptcy. Years of financial loss presented a roadblock to Apple's resurrection. One of the critical decisions Steve Jobs took to bring Apple back to life was to decrease the number of products from 350 to 10. Yes, you read that right. A reduction from 350 products to only 10 translated into a whopping 97 per cent of Apple's offerings gone. A bold move like this required courage, conviction and vision. But that one action of slashing 97 per cent of its offerings transformed Apple's fortunes. A year later, the company had moved out of the red zone. It had gone from losses worth $1.04 billion to a profit of $309 million.

What was the reason behind Steve Jobs's decision? By slashing the product line down to just a few core offerings, he wanted to make sure that the ten things Apple offered were the best. This philosophy helped Apple develop fewer yet revolutionary and straightforward products and services like the iPhone, iMac, iPad and iTunes. Their products were so ingenious and easy to use that even a child could use them. Apple's philosophy has made it the world's largest technology company and, more than anything, an aspirational brand that inspires business owners globally.

Steve Jobs went ahead and encouraged other leaders to adopt a more streamlined approach to their product lines.[18] On 21 April 2010, the editor of Fast Company, Robert Safain, interviewed the CEO and president of Nike, Mark Parker. Parker spoke about a phone call from Jobs which wholly altered his thinking for the better.

'Do you have any advice for me?' Parker had asked Jobs.

After a little pause, Jobs answered, '*Well, I do have some advice. Nike makes some of the best products in the world. Products people lust after. Absolutely beautiful, stunning products.*

---

[18] 'Steve Jobs' Advice to Nike: Get Rid of the Crappy Stuff', Fast Company, 16 September 2010, https://www.youtube.com/watch?v=SOCKp9eij3A.

But you also make a lot of crap. Just get rid of the crappy stuff and focus on the good stuff.'

His words profoundly impacted Parker. 'He was absolutely right. We have to edit,' he admitted to the audience present at the interview.

In both scenarios, we see how the 'Small is big' source code is about *saying no to many things that don't matter or contribute to progress.* When we say no to many things, we automatically begin to say yes to the select few priorities that positively impact our lives.

I can think of many successful companies, besides Apple, concentrating on a select few products and reaping huge profits. Some of the biggest multinationals today and global thought leaders invested all their effort and energy in building their business around a few products. Their goal was to provide a structured product line and ensure that what they offered were undeniably the best in class. This approach went a long way in making such organizations forces to reckon with.

Think of Crocs, among the most comfortable footwear you'll ever wear. Started in 2002, Crocs concentrated on making an empire out of one primary product: foam clog footwear. Channelling their attention on creating soft, comfortable, lightweight and odour-resistant shoes that worked well on land and water, the company revolutionized footwear and became a cultural symbol. The organization has managed to sell more than 700 million pairs. Their single-minded focus on innovation and one product line won the game for them and for their customers.

When you enjoy a long drive in your car or a breezy bicycle ride, chances are that your vehicle's tyres are from Michelin. For 132 years, Michelin has been serving customers one product: tyres. Yes, tyres ranging from those you see in bicycles to those used in agricultural equipment and aircraft. As of 2019, the organization was clocking revenues of €24.13 billion annually and was the second-largest tyre manufacturer globally.

In India, walk into any kitchen and you'll probably find an excellent example of a brand that made it big using only one product. In 1959, Hawkins Cooker Limited started servicing Indian households with their line of pressure cookers. Cut to 2021; the company now derives 80 per cent of its total revenue from pressure cookers and the remaining 20 per cent from ancillary cookware.

Having worked with bootstrapped and funded (Series A, B, C, D) start-ups, I understand that discontinuing a product is challenging for a company. Every product is the labour of the team's hard work, and everybody involved establishes an emotional connect with it. In difficult situations, this attachment to the product overrules discretion. But if one has to sustain profitable growth, cutting down the number of products is necessary sometimes. Reflecting on the following questions can help entrepreneurs and business leaders in exercising prudence when they consider rationalization of their product portfolio:

1. What are my current ongoing investments—people, technology, infrastructure, etc.—in this product?
2. What is the current financial contribution (to top line/ bottom line) from this product line?

3. What is the projected financial contribution (to top line/bottom line) from this product line?

Product rationalization can also be minimized or avoided by addressing a small set of problems. Let's observe the trajectory of technology giants like Amazon, Google, Facebook and YouTube.

Amazon, the world's biggest online retailer, started in 1994 with a simple purpose: to deliver books to any customer living anywhere. Jeff Bezos's research revealed that many books were unavailable offline and that bookstores took a long time to bring them to people. Many predicted that once book-selling giants such as Barnes and Nobles went online, it would signal the end of Amazon. But Jeff Bezos, who felt that his critics did not understand the potential of selling on the Internet, defeated stiff competition and continued to expand the scope of the website. More merchandise was put up for sale and, simultaneously, a system of recommendations and ratings put in place.

Founded in a college dormitory room, Sergey Brin and Larry Page began Google as an antidote to irrelevant Internet search results. They wanted to create a new search technology that did not just return a list of immaterial websites ranked according to how many times the search phrase was present in their content. Brin and Page aimed to build an information-aggregator search engine that yielded comprehensive results. Most importantly, each result would lead users to newer avenues of information. And, although Google now boasts an impressive and expansive product line, the search engine remains its core.

What was the one goal with which Google started? To simplify the act of looking for information on the Internet.

In 2004, when Mark Zuckerberg started writing the code for Facebook (called TheFacebook back then), he was surprised that Harvard University did not have an interactive online platform for students to communicate on. Up until then, Harvard had only a static online directory that offered no form of interactivity. Zuckerberg's goal was to create a site that crossed Harvard's private dormitories and brought together every student. From then until now, that is Facebook's primary aim; to connect people across the globe.

Chad Hurley, Stephen Chan and Jawed Karim realized that for non-tech experts there wasn't a video-sharing platform where users could upload videos they had made and enjoy a conversation about them. The trio wanted to create a video streaming platform which the new Internet users of the early 2000s would feel comfortable using without feeling overwhelmed by technology. And so was born YouTube, the most massive and frequently used video-sharing platform, which is today the source of income for millions of content creators globally.

What do you think is the common thread that connects each of these organizations and simultaneously resonates with the 'Small is big' source code in business? Look closely, and you'll find that each service provider mentioned above focuses on only a specific set of problems. Their operations aren't spread across a massive domain, covering ten different things. They all started with the dream of being solution providers to a particular kind of problem. While they did branch out later, their core remained an e-commerce website, a search engine, a social media network and a video-sharing platform. In the business world, the core area in which one operates is often referred to as a 'niche'. Operating within a niche has multiple advantages, the most significant being that the clientele thinks of the company as an expert when it comes to that niche. This image itself establishes excellent trust among consumers and attracts better prospects. The whole reason why niche services are essential can be understood if you think of the difference between a general physician and a specialist doctor. When you have a problem with your eyes, you'll visit an ophthalmologist rather than a general physician. We trust people and institutions with in-depth knowledge of a specific segment or a domain rather than someone who has fragmented information about many things. Each tech giant started small before making it big, as start-ups servicing a niche need.

Even in my personal experience, I have enjoyed the benefits of working on a niche product line. When I worked for large companies, getting meetings with senior executives was difficult and rare. Things changed since 2010, when I began to work with different start-ups that concentrated on solving one problem for a specific industry.

One start-up is addressing regulatory compliance for banks.

Another start-up is addressing customer experience for financial services.

Still another is addressing advanced analytics and customer experience for retail brands.

Because of their niche specializations and associated propositions, the start-ups I worked for gained business in countries without a physical office or a sales team in those places. Meeting a CMO, CEO, CFO or CDO (Chief Digital Officer) every week became a reality. All this happened because the start-ups were concentrating on servicing a specific problem within a specific industry segment. The size of the organizations didn't matter; their niche specializations did.

Learning Accelerator

1. What are the three niche problems you or your organization are solving for clients?

   a. _____

   b. _____

   c. _____

2. Which one of the three offers you a significant competitive advantage? Please put a tick against that one.

3. If you have to stop one product from among your multiple products, which one would you stop? In the following template, fill in each cell with either High, Medium or Low. This will guide you to make a decision.

	Product 1	Product 2	Product 3
Current Ongoing Investments			
Current Financial Contribution			
Projected Financial Contribution			

10

Concise and Captivating: Five Pointers for Crisp Business Presentations

'When deciding between giving a longer or shorter presentation, pick shorter. "I wish you had talked longer" are six words you'll seldom hear from audiences.'

—Sam Harrison, public speaker, trainer and author, *Creative Zing!*

How often in a week are you in a meeting, trying your best to concentrate on the presentation but failing because each slide has so much text? We've all been in that position more than once. This situation has often been described as 'Death by PowerPoint'. The audience feels bored and disengaged, even though they appear to be watching and listening to the presentation. So, why do we need to focus on shorter, more impactful presentations?

Is it only because they look better? No, there is much more to this. Crisp, exciting presentations are essential to keep your audience engaged and simultaneously be efficient for productive time management. The more concise and attractive your presentation, the faster people retain the information and the more effective will be your future discussions. The idea is to present material that can spark a conversation.

So, can we implement 'Small is big' to create captivating presentations? Is there a way to build an impactful presentation that perfectly expresses the message without distracting the audience with never-ending slides? In my experience, I have noticed five effective pointers that positively help streamline presentations and give you a final product that has a lasting impact on your audience.

Pointer 1: What is the one key message in your presentation?

Every presentation has a purpose. There is a central message that the presenter wants his or her audience to recognize and retain. The first guideline to keep in mind while building a presentation is what you want people to remember after the presentation. Once that critical point is clear, it becomes much easier to edit and pace the narrative. In my experience, repeating that *one* message many times and in different ways deepens audience understanding and improves memory recall.

Here are two examples of key messages:

Key message 1: For timely adherence to central bank regulatory requirements, you require a partner who can complete the project in five months and had implemented the same in at least ten banks.

Key message 2: For future-proof personalization experiences, you need an integrated platform that enables personalization for search, content and product recommendations.

Through the key messages mentioned above, the central communication that the presenter wishes to convey can be quickly identified. It is like a short pitch that hits the nail on the head and lays bare the presentation's objective at the outset.

Here's another pro tip. When drafting your key message, you can always turn to books to see how authors have created the titles and subtitles. It is an excellent way to understand how the crux of the matter in your presentation can be expressed in a few words. Here are a few for reference:

- *The Code of the Extraordinary Mind* (Vishen Lakhiani): 10 Unconventional Laws to Redefine Your Life and Succeed on Your Own Terms
- *The 4-Hour Work Week* (Timothy Ferriss): Escape the 9–5, Live Anywhere and Join the New Rich
- *The Ultimate Sales Accelerator* (Amit Agarwal): One Surprisingly Powerful Strategy to Create Epic Sales in Business and in Life

The next time you are creating a presentation, the following question will help in creating a powerful and clear message: *If my presentation was a book, what title and subtitle will I create?*

If you are having trouble building your key message, a helpful technique is to ask yourself: *If I was only given 20 per cent of the scheduled time, how will I serve and inspire my audience?*

When we plan content for a lesser duration, our presentation message becomes sharper.

Pointer 2: One message per slide

While this may seem an easy thing to do, our past experience with lengthy presentations makes this a complex task to implement in real life. Around ten years ago, one of my seniors told me that the first thing he reads in a presentation is each slide's headline. It gives him a quick overview of what is to follow. This made me understand the importance of a slide's headline and the need to keep it precise.

Think of the one-message-per-slide rule as writing a compelling headline for a newspaper article. You have a few words in hand. You have to learn how to convey the central point so the audience understands the discussion.

Let's say you are discussing revenue forecasts for 2021. The headline of your slide says, 'Asia's Revenue Projections for FY21'.

Place yourself in the audience's position. Can you understand anything substantial from the given information? Nothing much, right?

Now, consider another headline option:

'What are Asia's Sales Goals for FY21?

27 client logos with $4.7 million in order bookings'

Which one is more impactful? Of course, it's the second. That's because it gives a quick gist of what is to follow and achieves that without using heavy words.

An easy way to come up with clear headlines is to ask yourself a question, '*If I don't present the slide, will the audience get the gist of the slide by reading the headline?*'

Pointer 3: Six objects or less in one slide

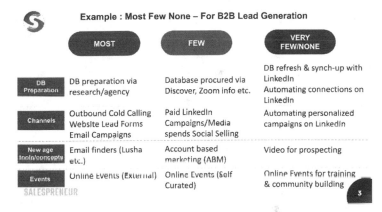

Fig. 10.1

Look at the slide above. Will you call it cluttered? Perhaps not. In fact, the information is presented in quite a structured and neat manner. However, is it an efficient slide? This is where it can fall short.

A slide may not look cluttered or disorganized, but can contain so much information that the viewer feels overwhelmed. Nothing dampens audience enthusiasm and involvement like a jam-packed slide. Sometimes we get so carried away with providing information we forget that *how we present* the data is as important as *what* the data is. The result is slides crammed with so many elements that the very sight of them is exhausting for the audience. They are unable to extract any valuable takeaways from what you are presenting.

In one of my favourite TED Talks, 'Death by PowerPoint',[19] David J.P. Phillips conducts a live experiment. He shows the audience a slide with ten balls, seven balls and five balls and asks them to nod once they had counted them. The time taken for the audience to count the ten balls, seven balls and five balls were 2 seconds, 1.2 seconds and 0.2 seconds, respectively. Philips noted how the cognitive process of counting seven balls required 500 per cent more time and energy than counting five balls. That is what he wanted his audience to keep in mind. It doesn't matter if you've created a fantastic PowerPoint. The moment there are seven or more objects on a slide, it requires people 500 per cent more energy and cognitive resources to understand and absorb what the slide is all about. For Phillips, the magic number is six. By limiting the number of points or areas to be addressed at six or less per slide, the audience has enough breathing space to engage with the presentation and not get distracted by the clutter on the slide.

---

[19] David J.P. Phillips, 'How to Avoid Death by PowerPoint', TEDxStockholmSalon, 14 April 2014, https://www.youtube.com/watch?v=Iwpi1Lm6dFo.

Pointer 4: Capitalize on contrast

While reading a book, we often highlight a section with a different colour or underline it with a pencil. When we refer to the book, the highlighted area contrasts with the parts that are not highlighted. This makes it easier for the reader to focus on and extract the key message from the larger text. This same principle applies to the art of creating PowerPoint presentations. This can be achieved using two simple tricks: *Bold and Grey* and *Annotations and Animations*.

Option 1: Bold and Grey

In the following images of slides which part of the picture comes to your notice first? It must be the writing in bold, because it stands out from the lighter text in grey.

THREE **EQ** ASPECTS WE WILL COVER TODAY

1.GRATITUDE

2.VISUALIZATION

3.SELF-TALK & SELF-PRAISE

SALESPRENEUR   4

Fig. 10.2

What we will cover today

Sales Sutra 1: The Magic quadrant of Go to Market (GTM) Excellence. Visualize your organization GTM strength in less than 1 min.

Sales Sutra 2: Metaphor, a sign of pure genius Become a Persuasion powerhouse using just two words.

Sales Sutra 3: The magic of one thing in Sales How to achieve more Sales by doing Less.

Sales Sutra 4: Mount Everest of Needs Decoding unmet and unknown needs of your customer

Sales Sutra 5: Most Few None, fastest and proven way to become a Trusted adviser

Sales Sutra 6: How to be a great storyteller in 4 simple steps

Sales Sutra 7: Are you selling to the buyer or to a user?

SALESPRENEUR

Fig. 10.3

Option 2: Annotations and Animations

When you look at the Fig. 10.4, it is no surprise that you first look at the dotted rectangles. These specific highlights are called annotations.

 We are using Metaphors all the time…..(Few more examples)

To highlight the enormity of a $1 trillion debt in simple words, the US President Reagan said in 1981

> "A trillion dollars would be a
> stack of thousand-dollar bills
> 67 miles high."

SALESPRENEUR

Fig. 10.4

An alternative and even more engaging way of using annotations is to employ the highlighting tools in PowerPoint or in remote meeting software like GoToMeeting and Zoom. A live annotation is a novel approach for audience engagement because of the surprise factor; your viewers aren't expecting it. In Fig. 10.4, we can use PowerPoint annotation capabilities to draw rectangles on the words 'a trillion dollars' and '67 miles high'.

 We are using Metaphors all the time…..(Few more examples)

To highlight the enormity of a $1 trillion debt in simple words, the US President Reagan said in 1981

"A trillion dollars would be a stack of thousand-dollar bills 67 miles high."

Fig. 10.5

Animations help us to pace our content better. Instead of introducing all of it at once, one can create animations to improve the speed and timing of introducing the content in our presentation. This creates a balance, enabling viewers to process the information and retain it better.

For example, I use the following animations to explain the Mount Everest of needs, a concept introduced in my book *The Ultimate Sales Accelerator.*

Sales Sutra 4 - Climbing 'Mount Everest of Needs'

Fig. 10.6

Sales Sutra 4 - Climbing 'Mount Everest of Needs'

Fig. 10.7

Sales Sutra 4 - Climbing 'Mount Everest of Needs'

Unserviced
neds

*Unknown
needs*

*Known needs:
Resistance to
change*

*Known needs:
Not met*

Serviced
needs

*Known needs:
That are met*

MOUNT EVEREST OF NEEDS

Fig. 10.8

Pointer 5:

Include images

The rationale behind including more images in a presentation is two-fold: first, it is to go easy on words; second, it helps in storytelling. Given below are two examples that use a combination of picture and one message.

Fig. 10.9

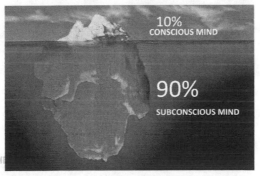

Fig. 10.10

So, is creating a concise, attractive and, above all, engaging PowerPoint presentation rocket science? No, it is anything but that. The idea is not to reduce the number of slides. It is to be mindful and aware about how to present your information so that the audience retains every bit of it. By leveraging the 'Small is big' source code and practising the five pointers discussed here, you take a step forward in becoming a more captivating creator and presenter. Here's a quick recap:

1. **Pointer 1:** What is the one key message in your presentation?
2. **Pointer 2:** One message per slide
3. **Pointer 3:** Six objects or less on one slide
4. **Pointer 4:** Capitalize on contrast using bold/grey, annotations, animations
5. **Pointer 5:** Include images

Learning Accelerator

Start by taking one presentation that you use at work and use the checklist below:

S. No.	Criteria	Response (Y/N)
1	Does the presentation have one key message?	
2	Does each slide contain only one key message?	
3	Do you have six or fewer than six objects per slide?	
4	Are you using annotation, animation, colour or size for contrast?	
5	Are you using images?	

Summary of 'Small is Big': Transforming Business

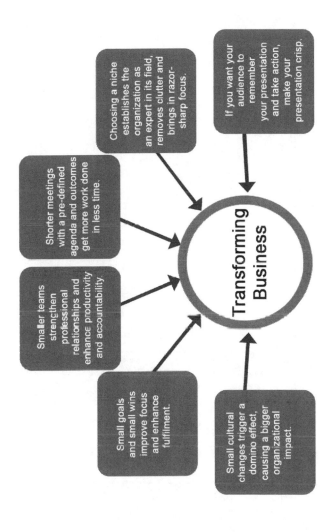

PART III

'Small Is Big'
Fuelling Productivity

11

What Is Productivity: Fusing Effectiveness and Efficiency

'Focus on being productive instead of busy.'

—Timothy Ferriss, entrepreneur and
author of *The 4-Hour Work Week*

How do we define productivity?
Mathematically, it is a ratio.

Productivity = Output/Input

Philosophically, productivity is about achieving more by doing less.

Action-wise, in the world of concrete, *implementable* actions, how can we be productive?

- By breaking a negative thought pattern.
- By developing a micro-habit, which will create a domino effect.
- By working on our negative resonances.

- By setting small goals and celebrating the small wins.
- By creating our niche and focusing on fewer products.
- By getting more done by means of a small team.
- By communicating our ideas in a shorter presentation.

Observe closely; you'll notice how similar they are. Each of the above saves time by harnessing the power of Small. Can the three dimensions of *mathematics, philosophy* and *action* be merged to give us a well-rounded insight into productivity?

If the denominator (input) in the mathematical ratio (productivity = output/input) is lowered, the resultant productivity will always increase. Isn't this similar to the philosophical perspective, which is about achieving more by doing less? Weren't all the actions discussed in the Life and Business section about maximizing gains while keeping everything simple? Whether mathematical, philosophical or action-oriented, each approach towards achieving productivity shares the exact crux of 'Small is big'.

So, how can we reduce our input and increase our productivity quotient? Surprisingly, the answer is simple. Input can be lowered by being *effective* and *efficient*. To improve productivity, we need to concentrate on these two parameters. A thought must have crossed your mind. Effectiveness and efficiency—how different are they? Don't we use the terms interchangeably? Yes, we do. However, there is a delicate line of difference that separates and connects them at the same time.

For me, *being effective is about choosing the right things from among the plethora of options available. Being efficient is about executing them to their fullest potential.*

Let's explore the concepts in greater detail, exploring what effectiveness and efficiency entail in our day-to-day lives.

Effectiveness	Efficiency
Focuses on why are we doing a specific action	Focuses on how the action needs to be done
Choosing and doing the right things	Doing things in the best possible manner
Subjective; comparatively challenging to measure	Objective; easier to measure
Related to vision and strategy	Related to execution

Let's look at a few examples of effectiveness and efficiency in business and life.

Business Examples of:

Effectiveness	Efficiency	Inefficiency
To decrease fatigue during pandemic times, a manager decreases the duration of reviews to 30 minutes from 60 minutes.	A manager uses the 3-point meeting template to define the inputs and prerequisites, agenda and output for each review. Every review is structured so that it is done within 30 minutes.	Informal reviews without any inputs and prerequisites, agenda or outcome defined. Reviews continue to stretch for 45–50 minutes.

Effectiveness	Efficiency	Inefficiency
To promote employee learning and development, an HR function launches an initiative of 40 hours of learning annually for every employee.	HR creates a tracking mechanism for measuring monthly learning hours for every employee. HR evangelizes the benefits of such sessions and finally assigns a 15 per cent annual appraisal to complete learning hours.	Informal set-up with no formal tracking mechanism and absence of alignment with performance management.

Life Examples of:

Effectiveness	Efficiency	Inefficiency
To increase bonding and to spend quality time together, a family adopts the habit of getting together for dinner every day.	Every day, the family has dinner together at the dining table before 7.30 p.m. During the meal, the members talk and share experiences for at least 15 minutes.	A family eats dinner together while watching TV. There is little conversation. Everyone is focused on what is happening on the screen.

Effectiveness	Efficiency	Inefficiency
To increase family time and create lifelong memories, a senior executive makes sure that he travels with his family once every quarter.	Every quarter, a senior executive takes a short vacation of at least four days. Every alternate quarter, his family goes on a week-long vacation. During that time, the executive does not check work emails or calls and dedicates all his time to his family.	During the family vacation, the executive is busy checking emails and taking calls. The family feels left out. The purpose of the holiday is defeated.

As given in above table, Effectiveness and Efficiency can be mapped to Strategy and Execution in both business and life. The table below shows that holistic productivity requires high effectiveness (strategy) and high efficiency (execution).

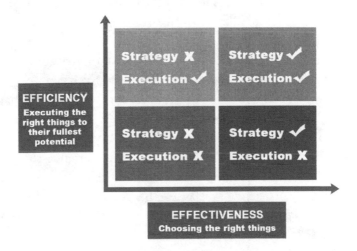

Fig. 11.1: The Magic Quadrant of Productivity

What is the relationship between effectiveness and efficiency? Peter Drucker, one of the greatest modern philosophers, whose writings have contributed significantly to business, said, *'Nothing is less productive than to make more efficient what should not be done at all.'*

Sounds complicated? No, it isn't! What Drucker highlights is that *effectiveness trumps efficiency.*

To understand this further, let's explore the following examples.

A start-up asks every employee to sign in and sign out at work every day. A deduction will be made from their salary if employees fail to do so. Reminders are issued, so employees apply for attendance regularization if they have forgotten to sign in or sign out.

What will be the impact of such an action? A start-up represents an open work culture and more flexibility than a traditional organization. By implementing such draconian measures for monitoring employee attendance, the organization sends out a poor message. If this initiative is diligently executed, it will instil fear of the company among the employees and also disregard for it.

At home, the family's adult members watch a film that is rated for age eighteen-plus with the children. When a few intimate scenes come on screen, an adult immediately fast-forwards those parts. It spoils the experience for the adults and invokes a particular curiosity among children that is beyond their years. When the film has been rated for adult viewing, how correct is it to watch it with children in the first place?

So, how can we balance efficiency and effectiveness to achieve productivity in what we do? I believe seven productivity tools are beautifully aligned with the 'Small is big' source code to help us be effective and efficient. They help fuel productivity, maximizing the returns received from small but concentrated efforts. Here's what they are:

1. The Pareto Principle
2. The Rule of Three
3. The One Thing
4. The Eisenhower Matrix
5. Power Time Capsules
6. Mind Maps
7. Checklists

Fig. 11.2: The Seven Tools of Productivity

12

The Seven Tools of Productivity

In the first half of this section on fuelling productivity, we explored the nuances of productivity itself. We spoke of effectiveness and efficiency, and how they are connected. We will now delve into the seven productivity tools that enable us to achieve more by doing less.

The Pareto Principle
(The 80–20 Rule)

*'Simplicity boils down to two steps:
Identify the essential, eliminate the rest.'*

—Leo Babauta

Vilfredo Pareto, an Italian economist, observed that only 80 per cent of Italy's land was owned by 20 per cent population. This was the beginning of the 80–20 Rule, renamed the 'Pareto Principle' by Joseph M. Duran. Duran was a management consultant who applied the rule to quality control. He found that 80 per cent of the issues were caused by only 20 per cent of the production defects.

The Pareto Principle states that 80 per cent of the effects stem from 20 per cent of the causes for most events. Now, what happens if we keep applying the Pareto Principle?

We start with 80 per cent of the effects coming from 20 per cent of the causes.

Applying the 80–20 rule to the above statement, we arrive at: *80 per cent of 80 per cent of the effects* are caused by *20 per cent of 20 per cent of the causes*.

This means 64 per cent of effects are caused by 4 per cent of the causes. Once again, 80 per cent of 64 per cent of the effects are caused by 20 per cent of 4 per cent of the causes. We then arrive at 51.2 per cent of the effects being caused by 0.8 per cent of the causes.

Or, *approximately 50 per cent of the effects are caused by 1 per cent of causes.*

Surprised at how so much can be caused by so little? You'll be amazed at how applicable the Pareto Principle is to real-life scenarios.

In October 2002, the CEO of Microsoft, Steve Ballmer, wrote in an internal three-page memo, 'About 20 per cent of the bugs cause 80 per cent of all errors, and—this is stunning to me—1 per cent of bugs caused half of all errors.'

In life and in business, we unknowingly encounter several examples of the Pareto Principle. As we discuss it, you'll see how they've escaped our notice for so long. Take the example of the primary business functions.

Finance

Approximately 20 per cent of customers contribute 80 per cent of the revenue.

Similarly, 20 per cent of the clients contribute to 80 per cent of the profits.

Sales

Approximately 20 per cent of sales owners drive 80 per cent of the sales.

Likewise, 20 per cent of prospective accounts in a region will drive 80 per cent of the market share.

Marketing

20 per cent of the marketing channels yield 80 per cent of the leads.

Around 20 per cent of the branding initiatives produce 80 per cent of the impact on brand visibility.

Operations

Approximately 20 per cent of the processes create 80 per cent of the efficiencies.

Around 20 per cent of a project's tasks pose 80 per cent of the risks to project completion.

Recruitment

Approximately 20 per cent of the hiring sources drive 80 per cent of the new hires.

While 80–20 is the numerical expression, the principle's crux is that the majority of effects result from only a small proportion of the causes. In my life and experience, I see the Pareto Principle prevalent in many ways.

In my professional career, which started in 1998, four to five years have created the most impact.

During my tenure in one of my organizations, I closed more than nine enterprise sales opportunities. Interestingly, only two contributed to more than 80 per cent of the total revenue.

While conducting interviews, I have used the Pareto Principle for effective division of time. I speak for 20 per cent of the interview time and let the candidate talk for the remaining 80 per cent of the time.

In my forty-five years of existence on earth till now, I have made many friends. Among them, there are only five with whom I speak regularly.

A family can bond over many activities. Out of the many options, a 20-minute walk with my wife and dinner with my children are honestly the two that give us the maximum joy.

It is evident that the Pareto Principle is beautifully aligned with the 'Small is big' source code. Common to both is the intrinsic belief that a small causative factor can create significant changes. Let us reflect on how to leverage the Pareto Principle and improve productivity levels in business and in our lives.

Learning Accelerator

1. List ten goals you wish to achieve in your current profession/job. Identify the top 20 per cent.

    1. _____

    2. _____

    3. _____

    4. _____

    5. _____

    6. _____

    7. _____

    8. _____

    9. _____

    10. _____

2. Name 10–20 friends you have in your life. Identify your relationship with the 20 per cent who give you the maximum joy and write how you can deepen the relationship.

    _____

    _____

    _____

    _____

    _____

The Rule of Three

'No one can remember more than three points.'

—Philip Crosby, American businessman and
author of *Quality is Free*

Have you experienced a situation where somebody has passionately presented many points, yet you don't remember anything from the presentation?

Have you experienced a situation where you have passionately presented so many ideas, yet they had no impact on people in terms of action on their part?

Why do you think this happens?

The rationale is simple: the moment you present too many items or ideas, it becomes complicated and difficult for people to understand and remember them. And if they can't remember your points, they can't connect with your thoughts or execute any action. We often use the phrase 'attention span of a goldfish' to describe a poor attention span. However, a study by Microsoft Corporation has found that average human attention has fallen from

12 seconds in 2000 to 8 seconds.[20] In fact, the goldfish has an attention span of 9 seconds. If you think about it, that phrase doesn't even apply any more! Our attention span is now weaker than that of a goldfish.

In that case, how do we know how much information to share? What is the cut-off point beyond which the listener is bound to get confused if you keep supplying more information?

In Latin, there is a phrase that goes '*Omne trium perfectum*', meaning, everything that comes in threes is perfect, or every set of three is complete. This forms the basis of the Rule of Three, which suggests that a trio of items is most likely to capture one's attention.

Look around you, and you'll find the Rule of Three in so many aspects of life.

Books: *The Three Musketeers, Three Men in a Boat, The Big Three in Economics*
TV channel names: MTV, CBS, CNN, HBO, ABC
Helpline numbers in different countries:

Country	Police	Ambulance	Fire
USA	911	911	911
India	100	102/108	101
UK	999 or 112	999 or 112	999 or 112

Number of recognitions for accomplishments: Look at sporting events such as the Olympics. They have three medals: gold, silver and bronze.

---

[20] K. McSpadden, 'You Now Have a Shorter Attention Span Than a Goldfish', *TIME*, 14 May 2015, https://time.com/3858309/attention-spans-goldfish/.

Public Speaking: Even when addressing a large crowd, using the Rule of Three will ensure that your audience can retain crucial information. While launching the iPhone in 2007,[21] Steve Jobs said:

> 'Well, today we're introducing three revolutionary products of this class. The first one is a widescreen iPod with touch controls. The second is a revolutionary mobile phone. And the third is a breakthrough Internet communications device. So, three things: a widescreen iPod with touch controls, a revolutionary mobile phone, and a breakthrough Internet communications device. An iPod, a phone, and an Internet communicator. An iPod, a phone . . . Are you getting it? These are not three separate devices, this is one device, and we are calling it iPhone. Today, Apple is going to reinvent the phone, and here it is.'

Jobs incorporated the Rule of Three quite often in his talks and work. In 2005, he was invited to Stanford to deliver the commencement address. He began with, 'Today, I want to tell you *three* stories from my life. That's it. No big deal. Just *three* stories.'

Unknown to us, we are hardwired to appreciate things that come in groups of three. It makes things easier and memorable.

Learning Accelerator

Attempt the following exercises to better experience the power of the Rule of Three:

1. Identify three things that you can do with your family every day for bonding.

    1. _____

    2. _____

    3. _____

2. List three personal strengths that have helped you in your professional growth.

    1. _____

    2. _____

    3. _____

3. For your next meeting, set up a three-point agenda.

    1. _____

    2. _____

    3. _____

The One Thing

'If there are nine rabbits on the ground, and if you want to catch one, just focus on one.'

—Jack Ma, business magnate
and philanthropist

Sometimes, life-changing things can happen to us—any time and anywhere. One such transformative event happened to me on 28 December 2017, during an ordinary cab ride. I was in Mumbai on the way to the airport after a client meeting. I began reflecting on the year that was coming to an end and the one about to begin. Suddenly, many things that I had always wanted to do flashed before my eyes.

- Meditation
- Reading the books that were gathering dust on my shelves
- Spending time with the kids
- Exercising daily
- Coming home early from office

- Writing
- Finishing my meals early

Does this list look familiar to you, especially around the time of New Year's? Yes, these are what we usually call New Year resolutions, and year after year they give us a lot of stress, don't they? Because as my list increased, my anxiety, too, was on a steady rise. Will I be able to do them this year? I had my apprehensions because in the past I hadn't been able to accomplish any of the tasks regularly. Yes, I was regularly irregular.

However, things were going to change. I believe that when we experience real yearning and intent, the Universe opens doors for us in ways we least expect. One such door was about to be opened, and that would change my life forever.

The door took the form of a book, *The One Thing*. I had heard its audio summary and finally started reading the book in December 2017. By that evening in the cab, I had already finished a few chapters and was captivated by its simplicity. The entire book is based on one simple and powerful question, called the 'Focusing Question'.

What is the one thing I can do, such that by doing it, everything else would be easier or unnecessary?

Let us go back to where we left off; the cab ride on 28 December 2017. In my desire to change my state of being regularly irregular, I asked myself the Focusing Question: *'What is the one habit I can develop in 2018, such that by developing it, everything else would become easier or unnecessary?'*

I was pleasantly surprised to see that my answer was relatively prompt: *'Start waking up early. Join the 5 a.m. club.'*

Sometimes it is wise to go with the flow rather than get into a lot of logical reasoning. I am glad that I went with the flow. On 2 January 2018, I woke up at 5 a.m. with the support of an alarm clock. I can't tell you how much my body resisted leaving the cosy blanket. The One Thing mindset empowered my mind to support my body. My mind said, 'It's only one thing. Just one thing— of waking up at 5 a.m. Let's give it a shot.' When there are fewer things to focus on, the mind becomes sharper and more cooperative. If it weren't for the fact that waking up early was the One Thing, I might have immediately gone back to bed! So, I woke up at 5 a.m.—and so much changed.

The first question that arose on my waking up early was: 'What do I do now?'

Reading was a prudent choice, and I resumed *The One Thing* from where I had left off in December 2017. After 20–30 minutes of reading, I checked the time. It was only 5.30 a.m. I then did a little yoga and meditation. I had my breakfast early and started work at around 8 a.m. Since I began my work early, I could finish it before my usual time. I had my dinner at 7 p.m. rather than at the usual 8.30 p.m. Post-dinner, I watched television with my kids and read them two bedtime stories. Everything was done by 9.15 p.m.! It was a remarkable change—to go to bed by 9.30 p.m. rather than at the usual 11 p.m. Knowing that it takes sixty-six days to form a new habit, I diligently woke up at five in the morning for the next sixty-six days. Over time, this routine became predictable. Waking up at 5 a.m. made space for many new things in my day. Practising gratitude, cycling and writing were three new things that I started, which I continue to enjoy to date.

Practising gratitude gave me a sense of fulfilment.

Cycling at sunrise is an excellent form of physical and mental exercise and gave me the chance to relive childhood memories.

Writing led me to publish my first book, *The Ultimate Sales Accelerator: One Surprisingly Powerful Strategy to Create EPIC Sales in Business and Life,* in July 2019. The book's concept was also inspired by the focusing question from *The One Thing* that I asked myself in July 2018 over breakfast with my wife:

If somebody asked me, what is the one thing that contributed the maximum to my success in sales, what would I respond?

Now you must be wondering, 'All this sounds good. But where is the magic?'

If you go back to the beginning of the section, you'll see that long list of things I wanted to achieve and how anxious I was about not being able to see them through. But when I decided to do just the one thing of waking up at 5 a.m., everything else fell into place. All the other stuff got done. Magical, isn't it? The One Thing certainly creates a domino effect.

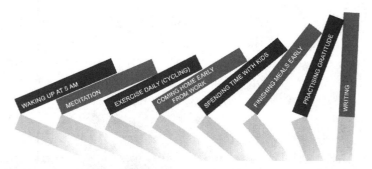

Fig. 12.1: The Domino Effect with the One Thing

At this stage, a thought must have crossed your mind. The Pareto Principle, the Rule of Three and The One Thing are all about streamlining many things to arrive at the most important few. So, how do we understand which approach to apply to arrive at the best results?

Interestingly, the answer lies in the thread of commonality among the three. The Pareto Principle, the Rule of Three and The One Thing all focus on achieving more by doing less.

The Pareto Principle is excellent if one is handling large data sets, especially when the number of items crosses twenty.

The Rule of Three helps address wavering attention by leveraging the human mind's bias towards groups of three.

The One Thing represents the highest level of clarity and confidence. It is comparatively harder when compared to the above two, yet it goes a long way in developing one's intuitive ability.

Let's say your CEO asks you to find a list of things to help improve sales. You work with functions and identify thirty items that will improve sales. After making a list of those thirty things, you apply the 80–20 rule to get six high-impact items. You then use the Rule of Three to identify three high-priority items among those six. You then apply The One Thing rule to select the highest-priority item from among the three as the one item that can vastly improve sales. That's your One Thing. These three tools help you focus on less to achieve more, helping you choose the most effective item from among thirty items that you think can advance sales. It enables us to achieve big results by concentrating on a few key things.

Learning Accelerator

1. What's the one habit I can develop this year to improve
    my mental wellness and overall well-being?

    _____

    _____

    _____

2. I work in <name of the function>. What's the one
    activity I can stop doing in the department from this
    quarter for better results?

    _____

    _____

    _____

The Eisenhower Matrix

*'What is important is seldom urgent, and
what is urgent is seldom important.'*

—Dwight D. Eisenhower,
34th president, USA

Dwight Eisenhower was the thirty-fourth president of the USA. He was a statesman par excellence, serving in critical positions—as a five-star general in the US Army, as president of Columbia University and as the first supreme commander of NATO—before he assumed the presidency.

All of you must be thinking, 'That must have been a busy man.'

But here's a fascinating insight into the life of Eisenhower. While holding such senior positions, he found the time to pursue hobbies like golfing and oil painting. You can sense that Eisenhower was a very productive person. Eisenhower shared his wisdom by introducing the Eisenhower Matrix, a productivity tool to prioritize important things and to remove the clutter from one's life. The mechanism involved two paraments: *Urgent* and *Important*.

What do Urgent and Important Entail?

Urgent covers any time-sensitive deliverables that need immediate attention. The simplest way to filter what is urgent from what is not is by asking yourself: 'If I don't do this task now, will I lose significantly?'

Important items are those that fuel holistic growth. To assess which tasks are essential, the most uncomplicated filtering question is, 'If I do this task, will I evolve and gain holistically?'

The Eisenhower Matrix has four quadrants, with urgency and importance being the sieving measures.

1. *Urgent* and *Important*: Execute such tasks immediately, like dealing with a health emergency.
2. *Urgent* but *Not Important*: Delegate these tasks, like booking a flight for business travel the next day.
3. *Important* but *Not Urgent*: Plan and schedule well in time, like focusing on mental wellness.
4. *Not Important* and *Not Urgent*: Eliminate these tasks, like logging into your social media accounts many times in the day.

An Eisenhower Matrix looks something like this:

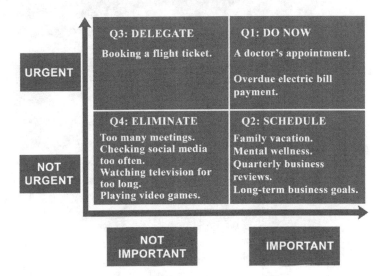

Fig. 12.2: An Eisenhower Matrix

In this manner, we can create valuable matrices for ensuring that we know where to align our focus. The following is an Eisenhower Matrix that I have used to achieve higher productivity in personal finance.

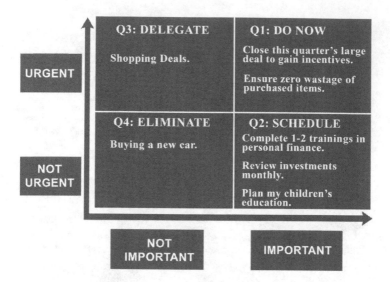

Fig. 12.3: An Eisenhower Matrix for Personal Finance

Most of you will assume that Quadrant 1, Urgent and Important, must be the central one of the four. At a cursory and logical level, you are correct. However, if you delve deeper and internalize the matrix's spirit, you'll realize that it is Quadrant 2, Important but Not Urgent, that needs to be our highest priority. Why is that so?

Let's consider mental wellness.

Person A doesn't exercise or meditate. He plays video games for 2 hours and watches television for 3 hours daily. He is pursuing something in Quadrant 4. If this continues, person A will face a severe health problem and move to Quadrant 1, where a health emergency needs immediate attention. A simple way not to get into this situation would have been assigning exercise and meditation to Quadrant 2.

Person B exercises and meditates for 45 minutes a day. He is in Quadrant 2. Person B will not move to Quadrant 1 because of good planning and solid execution. Due to constant repetition, exercise and meditation will have become his habit.

By scheduling and implementing items in Quadrant 2, we minimize tasks in the Urgent and Important zone. When Quadrant 2 is not completed in time, things become urgent and move to Quadrant 1. The more the things that pile up in Quadrant 1, the more stressful our lives become. Who likes to deal with a crisis or face health emergencies?

The COVID-19 pandemic was a great reminder of this, when a large section of society was impacted as a result of their low immunity. It forced us to move mental wellness and holistic health to Quadrant 2.

While I believe that Quadrant 2 is the most important one, you may have a different idea. I realized this while talking to my fifteen-year-old son, Tanish. One morning, while we were discussing the Eisenhower Matrix, I asked him, 'Which is the most important quadrant for you?'

Immediately he answered, 'Quadrant 4; Not Urgent and Not Important.'

His reply both surprised and intrigued me. 'Okay, why is that so?'

Tanish said, 'If we remove Quadrant 4, we are removing what is Not Urgent and Not Important. It will give us so much time for focusing on what is urgent and important?'

With pride in my eyes and joy in my heart, I agreed with him. Wisdom can come from anywhere, and at that moment my fifteen-year-old son had become my guru.

The Eisenhower Matrix is built on the idea that our lives become more manageable by defining tasks based on their urgency and importance. It paints a crystal-clear image of which items need immediate attention, which can be fulfilled in a phased manner, and which are unnecessary. The four quadrants improve decision making, develop clarity and remove clutter. This is the essence of 'Small is big'.

Adopting a Three-day Workweek

An inspirational story of how an individual achieved contentment by knowing what is *important* for happiness and by *eliminating* clutter is that of Neeraj Deginal. The author of *Zero Debt: Break the Debt Cycle and Reclaim your Life*, Neeraj adopted an almost radical approach. I've enjoyed interacting with Neeraj, and he has been kind enough to share his aspirational story for this book.

In 2014, Neeraj was wholly debt-free and was in the process of simplifying his life. His goal was simple: to maximize the time he could spend with his daughter and family and explore new opportunities. This desire prompted in him an interesting idea; he prepared a plan for working only three days a week for his organization with a 30 per cent cut in salary. Fortunately, his boss agreed to his proposal. All of this could happen because of the following reasons:

- A salary cut of 30 per cent would still sustain his earlier lifestyle.
- He wanted lower stress levels in life.
- He wished to spend more time with family and friends.
- He wished to spend time exploring other opportunities.

Ever since adopting a three-day workweek, Neeraj has been enjoying a wonderful life. In 2015, he and his wife welcomed their second daughter, and for that milestone and for everything else, he had all the time he needed! All this could happen because Neeraj prioritized what was important for him and identified what could be done away with.

Learning Accelerator

Plan your day at work and evaluate your tasks using the Eisenhower Matrix.

	NOT IMPORTANT	IMPORTANT
URGENT	Q3 : DELEGATE	Q1 : DO NOW
NOT URGENT	Q4 : ELIMINATE	Q2 : SCHEDULE

Power Time Capsules

'If you split your day into ten-minute increments, and
you try to waste as few of those ten-minute increments
as possible, you'll be amazed at what you can get done.'

—Ingvar Kamprad, founder of IKEA

What Can you Achieve in One Second?

Here's another question: What can be achieved in one-hundredth of a second? It was with a margin of one-hundredth of a second that Michael Phelps, one of the most famous swimmers in history, won one of his celebrated Olympic gold medals. The 2008 Beijing Olympics witnessed one of the most historic moments in sport when Michael Phelps clinched the gold after beating Milorad Cavic by 0.01 seconds. While Phelps finished the 100 m butterfly at 50.58 seconds, Cavic took the silver medal at 50.59 seconds. Such a happening makes one wonder that if 0.01 seconds can determine the gold medal at the Olympics, what are the possibilities that can be unlocked if a day is divided into smaller, concentrated segments? What can be achieved if we focus our attention on smaller units of time than we do currently?

In today's world we are constantly surrounded by distractions, such as our constant urge to check social media, leading to a decreasing attention span, or making multiple commitments. These trends have a definite impact on our ability to concentrate. In such a situation, how can we increase our focus?

Segmenting a day into small, power time capsules can promise us noteworthy results. A power time capsule divides time into small brackets, ranging from 5 minutes to 30 minutes. The goal is that during each time capsule our focus should be razor sharp and wholly invested in the work that we are doing. This significantly reduces the chance of interruptions and distractions.

In this regard, the Pomodoro Technique[22] is also a powerful way to implement power time capsules. It is a simple productivity technique invented by Francesco Cirillo in the 1980s. It follows these easy steps:

1. Choose one specific task.
2. Set a timer for 25 minutes.
3. Work on the task for 25 minutes dedicatedly without any distraction.
4. Take a 5-minute break.

---

[22] F. Cirillo, (n.d.). 'The Pomodoro Technique®—proudly developed by Francesco Cirillo', Cirillo Consulting GmbH, https://francescocirillo.com/pages/pomodoro-technique.

5. After four consecutive Pomodoro time capsules, take a more extensive break of 20 minutes.

Simple steps, isn't it? Notice the 5-minute breaks? They serve a two-fold purpose. Firstly, they help the mind to rejuvenate. Secondly, 5-minute breaks implicitly create a mindset of celebration and gratitude. They enable the person to feel resourceful and further their readiness for the next Pomodoro time capsule.

If you wonder why we aren't focusing on a time capsule greater than 30 minutes, that's because a shorter time frame increases focus, eliminates boredom and minimizes distraction. I use 25-minute time capsules to improve my reading experience. I set the timer for 25 minutes and read without a break. After the 25-minute period is over, I enjoy a short 5-minute break and see how I feel. In the next 5 minutes, I write three to five things I learnt in the 25-minutes of reading.

In the business context, I have used power time capsules for shorter (<= 30 minutes) meetings; something we discussed in part 2 of this book.

Learning Accelerator

In the given scenarios, think about where can you apply a power time capsule of 5 minutes to 30 minutes:
- ☐ Official meetings
- ☐ Reading
- ☐ Working on a project, presentation or assignment.
- ☐ Vacationing
- ☐ Watching a film

Among the ones you have selected, highlight the item that is highest in terms of priority for implementation.

Mind Maps

'Mind maps offer the easiest way to get information into the brain as well as to take information out of it.'

—Tony Buzan, author, educational consultant and inventor of Mind Mapping

Until you taste the food, you can't tell whether it is good or bad. Do you agree with this statement? My experience with mind maps was something like this. I was aware of their benefits and power yet never explored the concept in detail. In 2020, I read Tony Buzan's life-changing book *Mind Map Mastery*. That is when I started realizing the power that lay in this tool. Mind maps are an excellent tool if you are drawn to exploring powerful ideas and their easy execution in 10–30 minutes.

So, what is a mind map? It is a revolutionary thinking tool that helps one process information, develop new ideas and strengthen one's memory. It activates the entire brain, engaging both the brain's logical left side and the creative right side.

Creating a mind map involves a set of simple, easy-to-follow steps. All you need is paper and a bunch of coloured pens.

1. Place a blank sheet of paper on a table. It should be in landscape orientation.
2. Draw a *central image* to represent the topic. Use a minimum of three colours and put a label (short description) on the image
3. Create branches that stem from the central image.
    *   Use a different colour for each branch.
    *   Write a word or image on each branch, representing the branch idea.
    *   Let the length of the branch be the same as the length of the word on it.
4. Create *secondary level* shoots from each branch. If required, create sub-branches from these shoots. Put a word or image on each secondary-level shoot that describes the idea of the shoot.

Mind mapping engages both sides of the brain. Colour relates to the right side of the brain, whereas words are associated with the rational left hemisphere.

It isn't enough that we only read about mind mapping. For instance, I unlocked the power of mind maps once I started practising them. While reading the book on mind mapping, I created more than twenty mind maps and continued the practice even after I finished reading the book.

I created mind maps for my company corporate deck, for the metrics required for GTM functions, for my holistic health, quarterly planning and virtual selling. Before writing this book, I created a mind map for this book as well. Mind maps are a magical tool in more ways than one. With mind maps, I benefited in the following ways:

1. I could find big ideas in a short period of time. I created some mind maps in under 5 minutes, never taking more than 30 minutes for one. That helped me keep things simple.
2. Mind maps helped me in structuring my thoughts, making planning easier.
3. Mind maps enabled me to execute actions in reality that I would have never thought of previously. This helped me harness my creativity and spontaneity.

Refer to Fig. 12.4 and 12.5 for two examples of the many mind maps I have made for structuring my thoughts.

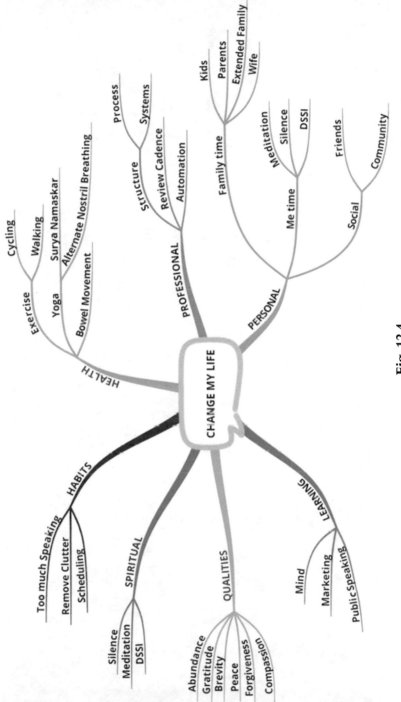

Fig. 12.4

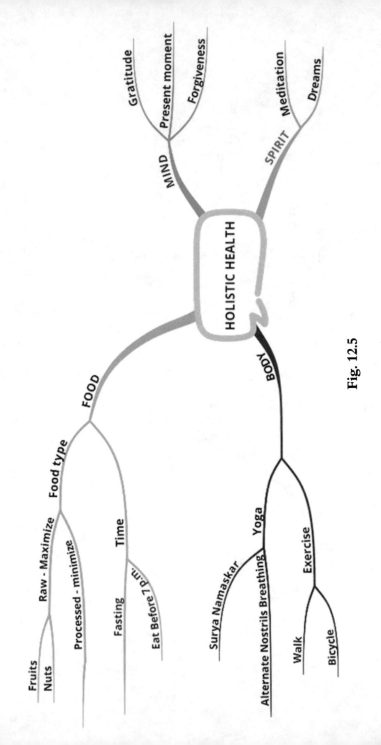

Fig. 12.5

Learning Accelerator

1. Give yourself minimum 10 minutes to create a mind map. Think of how you want to structure your week and the essential things you wish to do.

2. Now, following the four steps given earlier, create a weekly planner mind map on a sheet of paper.

3. Review your mind map.

Congratulations, your first mind map is ready!

Checklists

*'Checklists seem to be able to defend anyone, even the
experienced, against failure in many more tasks than
we realized. They provide a kind of cognitive net.
They catch mental flaws inherent in all of us—flaws of
memory and attention and thoroughness. And because
they do, they raise wide, unexpected possibilities.'*

—Atul Gawande, author of
The Checklist Manifesto

What is the first thought that comes to mind when
you think of checklists? Is it grocery shopping?
That's because grocery shopping lists are a great way of
being effective and efficient.

I live near a village and cycle to the local shops to
purchase my groceries and other household goods. Earlier,
I would memorize what I needed to buy. As a result, I
would forget many items, though I would buy most of
them. When I returned, my wife would ask, *'Where are the
AAA batteries and carrots?'*

I would say, 'Oh, I forgot' and, with a sense of frustration, go back to the market and buy whatever I had forgotten.

Does this situation seem familiar to you? What was happening here?

Right at the beginning, we had discussed how effectiveness consists in doing the right things, and efficiency in doing something right.

Was my wife effective in giving me the list of groceries? Yes.

Was memory the most effective way of remembering all that needed to be bought? No.

Did it lead to efficiency? No.

It took me 20 minutes to shop, but another 10 minutes were added to this because I had to return to the shop to get what I had forgotten. This caused an inefficiency of 50 per cent.

Checklists completely changed this. When I buy household items, I ensure that I carry a list of everything I need to purchase. The result has been fulfilling, because almost every time I go, I now return home with everything we need. Checklists have improved both my effectiveness and efficiency.

Checklists are a powerful productivity tool, not only for use in our day-to-day lives but also in life-sustaining professions such as medicine, aviation, and even business. Dr Atul Gawande, author of *The Checklist Manifesto*, believes that checklists not only offer the chance for verification but are symbolic of a kind of discipline aimed at higher performance.

In 2008, the World Health Organization (WHO) launched an initiative called 'Safe Surgery Saves Lives', where the organization introduced a medical checklist (Fig. 12.6) in conjunction with Dr Gawande. The checklist aimed to provide teams with highly efficient and easy priority checks, giving them a framework that would improve teamwork and communication and ensure high consistency in ensuring patient safety during surgery.

The results of the checklist implementation were startling and remarkable. In a pilot study, Dr Gawande's team prospectively observed more than 3000 patients before the introduction of the checklist and about 4000 patients after the implementation. They measured the degree of surgical complication or mortality up to thirty days after the surgery or up until discharge. The study was conducted in four hospitals in low to middle-income nations and four hospitals in higher-income countries.

It was found that the overall rate of death before the checklist came into the picture was 1.5 per cent. After the list was executed, this fell to 0.8 per cent! Moreover, in-patient complications also declined, from 11 per cent to 7 per cent after the checklist was introduced. As a measure of adherence to the checklist, six safety indicators, like pre-incision antibiotics, swab counts and routine anaesthetic checks, showed a performance increase from 34.2 per cent pre-checklist to 56.7 per cent post-checklist.

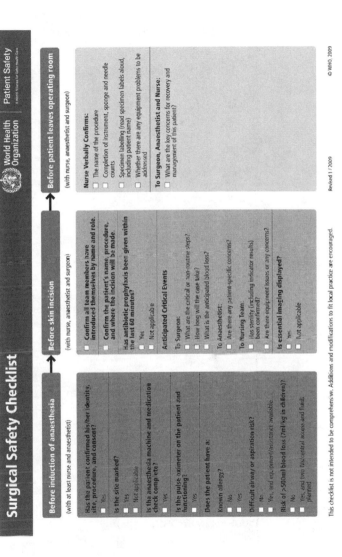

Fig. 12.6

Source: https://www.who.int/teams/integrated-health-services/patient-safety/research/safe-surgery/tool-and-resources

Even in business functions like sales, checklists can prove to be a great way of getting work done in a structured manner. I often find myself using the famous MEDDIC checklist. It is a sales methodology developed by Jack Napoli and Dick Dunkel. During their tenure at PTC Corporation in the mid-nineties, they used this framework to grow revenues from $300 million to $1 billion in just four years.

MEDDIC	What it means in business
M: Metrics	Identifying the key metrics to measure the economic impact of any solution being implemented.
E: Economic Buyer	The person who is the signing authority and assigns the budget for this solution.
D: Decision Criteria	Criteria—such as technical, functional and organizational stability—that are used to select and compare vendor offerings.
D: Decision Process	The process used to select vendor offerings. This includes clarity on events, timelines and people.
I: Identify pain	What are the known and unknown needs that have to be addressed by means of this solution? What happens if they are not addressed?
C: Champion	Some person within the buyer team who benefits from the solution and advocates it within the buyer organization.

I have significantly benefited from the MEDDIC checklist because of its inherent simplicity. It does not lead to a vast list of complicated steps that can overwhelm the user. It is easy, effective and efficient.

Alongside such powerful pre-designed checklists, we must make our own so that day-to-day living becomes more comfortable. It is a misconception that checklists always need to involve a long index of items. Remember, 'Small is big'. Even short ones are very effective. For example, there is a three-point daily checklist I used for my overall well-being:

Did I do my best to express my gratitude?
Did I meditate for 30 minutes?
Did I wake up at 5 a.m.?

It's short and has only three items, but helps me keep track of my holistic health on a day-to-day basis.

Even professionally, checklists are a great way to ensure that you exude the right vibe on official platforms. For example, we're all on LinkedIn, and it is imperative to create an excellent profile. For that, the following checklist can be quite helpful as it covers all aspects of what makes for a strong LinkedIn presence:

Criteria	Yes/No
Does my profile photo look professional, and do I have a pleasant expression on my face?	
Am I using a background banner?	
Do the profile headlines demonstrate how I am serving my target audience?	

Criteria	Yes/No
Do I have content in the *Featured* section?	
Is the description in the *About* section written in first person?	
Have I listed all my work assignments and education credentials?	
Do I have more than ten recommendations?	

In fact, checklists are an excellent tool to evaluate your knowledge in any field.

If you wish to assess an individual's mastery and expertise in something, ask him/her to create a checklist.

If you want to assess your own expertise and mastery in an area, create a checklist for that field.

If you want to develop your expertise and mastery in any area, create a checklist for that domain.

The rationale is simple and powerful. Creating a checklist is the simplest form of exercise for the brain, demonstrating and bringing forth a person's expertise and clarity.

The final question that arises is, how do we build an effective checklist? Think of it this way: you jot down everything you need or want to do, and the list can become so long that it overwhelms you and makes you anxious about whether you can attain your goal. Hence, it is essential to build a checklist that helps you achieve your tasks without overpowering you.

For that, I am sharing five characteristics of a practical checklist:

1. **Size:** The checklist fits into one page. According to Atul Gawande, author of *The Checklist Manifesto*, only five to nine critical items must make it to the checklist.
2. **Language:** Use simple and straightforward language that can be easily understood by you and anyone else who will be referring to it.
3. **Review:** Have Y/N or small checkboxes against each item so they can be ticked off upon completion of the task.
4. **Scope:** Try your best to make checklists for a specific requirement and not with a broad-based agenda. For example, a hiring checklist for evaluating project manager profiles is a detailed, need-based checklist. But making a checklist to assess the efficacy of the human resources function is broad and quite vague.
5. **Refine:** Checklists are not stagnant. They have to be reviewed and refined periodically to remain updated with what has to be done.

As you can see, checklists are one of the most underrated tools that guarantee productivity. They are easy to make, require next to no investment on your part except perhaps paper or an app on your phone, truly capturing the spirit of 'Small is big'.

Learning Accelerator

1. Please use the LinkedIn checklist given in this chapter to assess your LinkedIn profile.

Criteria	Yes/No
Does my profile photo look professional, and do I have a pleasant expression on my face?	
Am I using a background banner?	
Do the profile headlines demonstrate how I am serving my target audience?	
Do I have content in the *Featured* section?	
Is the description in the *About* section written in first person?	
Have I listed all my work assignments and education credentials?	
Do I have more than ten recommendations?	

2. Please create a checklist for any one of the following areas:
   a. hiring checklist for any particular position
   b. review checklist of any one client artifact that you create for your clients
   c. checklist for upcoming vacation

Summary of 'Small is Big': Fuelling Productivity

Right at the outset in this section, we defined productivity as the amalgamation of effectiveness and efficiency: Productivity = Effectiveness + Efficiency. Now that we have discussed the seven productivity tools, let's see how each contributes to the two dimensions.

Seven Tools of Productivity	Effectiveness (Choosing the Right Things)	Efficiency (Doing Things Right)
The Pareto Principle	✓	
The Rule of Three	✓	
The One Thing	✓	
The Eisenhower Matrix	✓	
Power Time Capsules	✓	✓
Mind Maps	✓	✓
Checklists	✓	✓

This table gives us an insight into how the seven tools are interconnected in terms of effectiveness and efficiency.

Now, you have probably noticed that except for Power Time Capsules, Mind Maps and Checklists, the remaining five tools tick only one of the two boxes. So, how are all seven tools related to both effectiveness and efficiency?

The answer lies at a deeper level. While the Pareto Principle, the Rule of Three, The One Thing and the Eisenhower Matrix primarily focus on effectiveness (choosing the right things from among many options), they significantly aid efficiency (as one gets to execute the chosen few activities in the best way). That's because when you select only the most crucial priorities you have fewer things to accomplish, which improves your performance.

Once the essential items are identified, power time capsules focus on execution by leveraging time as an asset.

Detailed mind maps provide information on both strategy and execution.

Checklists enable us to create small lists of things we need to do and use that as a framework to ensure effective execution.

The seven productivity tools help us *prioritize*, *optimize* and *simplify* the number of deliverables we have in business and in life.

To *prioritize* means to focus on a small set of things that matter and remove the distractions.

To *optimize* means to focus on shorter time intervals of action to aid faster execution.

To *simplify* means to break down complex matters in a way that brings structure and clarity to our activities.

Doesn't all this resonate deeply with the core of 'Small is big'—the source code of inspiring *big* changes by implementing *small* and decisive actions?

Epilogue

The Most Important Person

Amongst the 7.7 billion people on earth, who is the most important person for you?

When you reflect upon this question, a few names and pictures will come to your mind.
Your father.
Your mother.
Your partner.
Your child.
Your friend.
Your spiritual master.

....
....
....

Whom did you choose? If you chose yourself, congratulations. How many people consider themselves as the most crucial individual in their lives?

We are on earth for one reason. That reason is to *develop qualities*. The earth is a beautiful school that empowers us by helping us build qualities in ourselves. However, such is the way of the world that we often neglect our personal growth and fail to understand its value as we are too caught up in paying attention to our families, our companies or our teams. Now, you may ask me, 'I am just one person. What can a single person among the 7.7 billion people living on earth achieve?'

Friends, the world is full of instances where we see one person exhibiting the strength and power to produce tremendous impact.

Mahatma Gandhi created a powerful movement based on non-violence, which ultimately led India to independence after centuries of foreign rule.

Mother Teresa inspired millions by looking after the less fortunate and teaching the world the power of unconditional love and service.

Steve Jobs and his revolutionary vision pioneered path-breaking technologies that changed the face of music, software and so many other industries in the world.

Like Gandhi, Steve Jobs and Mother Teresa, you can also be a person who can create an immense impact in the world. *The most important person for each of us is ourselves, and it is time to work on our own personal, professional and spiritual growth.*

To work on ourselves, we need to focus on our thoughts, micro-habits and resonances.

To work on ourselves, we need to know how small, ground-level changes in our professional approach can produce a domino effect and positively change the work environment.

To work on ourselves, we need to learn how to be both effective (choosing the right options from among the many) and efficient (executing the selected items in the best possible manner).

Through this interconnected alignment of life, business and productivity, and by implementing the principle of 'Small is big', we learn how to invest our energies for our personal growth. When we grow in a way that makes us content, happiness is bound to illuminate our lives.

People say that to be happy, an individual needs to find his or her *purpose*. The word *purpose* can be quite daunting, and attempting to find it even more so. While, at a deeper level, the purpose of our lives to develop qualities, we can be more specific and find concrete, executable actions that put us on the path of self-transformation. Let me share two exercises that can help you in this journey.

Exercise 1

Answer the following questions:

If time and money were not an issue:

1. What are the things I would like to *experience* in life?
2. What *skills* would I like to learn for my growth?
3. What would I want to *contribute* to the larger community?

This powerful exercise by Vishen Lakhiani,[23] founder of MindValley, is from one of his YouTube videos 'The Three Most Important Questions to Ask Yourself'. In 2016, I did this exercise, and the most noteworthy points in my answers were 'Finish a 10-Day Vipassana Meditation' and 'Write a book'. The former came under *experiences* and the latter under *contribution*. Thankfully, I was able to complete both, which brought me a wonderful sense of healing, joy and fulfilment.

It is your turn now. What are your answers to the three questions?

Exercise 2

How would your epitaph read?

An epitaph is a short statement, commonly inscribed on a tombstone or read as part of a funeral oration, for or about a deceased person. An epitaph is meant to symbolize one's entire life in just a few words. Therefore, as a concept, it is most definitely aligned with 'Small is big'.

You must be familiar with the Nobel Prize, the world's most coveted honour awarded to people who have made exemplary contributions to physics, chemistry, medicine, literature and the promotion of peace. The prize is named after Alfred Nobel, a famous scientist. However, what you will be surprised to know

---

[23] 'The 3 Most Important Questions to Ask Yourself', Life at MindValley, 3 October 2012, https://www.youtube.com/watch?v=f8eU5Pc-y0g

is the list of inventions credited to his name. Alfred Nobel was an expert in explosives and designed a detonator, blasting cap and dynamite . . . all capable of mass destruction.

In 1888, Alfred Nobel's brother Ludvig passed away. However, a French newspaper mistakenly published a report announcing that Alfred Nobel had died. The headline read *'Le Marchand de la mort est mort.'* That translates into 'The Merchant of Death is Dead.'

The headline was almost like an epitaph and served as a harsh reminder to Alfred Nobel about his legacy's negative nature. Moreover, the article described Nobel as a man who had made his fortune by finding faster ways to kill people. Reading it, Nobel realized there was an urgent need to rehabilitate his image and create a positive legacy for the world to remember.

In his will, Alfred Nobel donated most of his wealth to the Nobel Foundation. Nobel now lives on, not as a merchant of death but as an advocate of innovation, progress and peace.

This anecdote made me think about how epitaphs can act as a powerful way to determine the purpose of one's life. Yes, it is closely associated with death, and thinking about your epitaph can be fearful. However, as in the case of Alfred Nobel, it can act as a catalyst for transformation.

My epitaph would read:

Amit Agarwal

Teacher at heart, Student at mind
and Warrior in action, who
Served *with*
Authenticity,
Love,
Expertise *and a*
Smile.

What would your epitaph say? Take a moment and write your epitaph. You may close your eyes for a powerful experience. Reading your epitaph every day can remind you how to live today so you can create a memorable legacy. This small exercise can catalyse action and initiate a significant transformation for you.

In a world of 7.7 billion people, imagine if *each* one of us works diligently on ourselves.

Newer patterns of thought, micro-habits and resonances will emerge.

This, in turn, will create a domino effect of universal fulfilment, productivity and extraordinary results. It starts with each of us adopting the source code—'Small is big'.

'Know yourself, and you will know the Universe.'

—Universe/City Mikael (UCM)
Teaching & Research Centre

References

I am grateful to all the sources of knowledge that helped me communicate the all-encompassing nature of 'Small is big'.

CHAPTER 2

The Journey of a Thought

- Masaru Emoto—Office Masaru Emoto. (n.d.). Accessed 19 March 2021, https://www.masaru-emoto. net/en/masaru/.
- 'Dr Masaru Emoto and Water Consciousness,' The Wellness Enterprise, accessed 28 February 2021, https://thewellnessenterprise.com/emoto/.

CHAPTER 3

Micro-Habits and their Associated Domino Effect

- www.satvicmovement.org, https://youtube.com/c/ SatvicMovement.
- Clear, J., 'How Long Does It Actually Take to Form a New Habit? (Backed by Science)', https://jamesclear. com/new-habit.

- 'Need to Form a New Habit? Give Yourself at least 66 Days', PsychCentral, https://psychcentral.com/blog/need-to-form-a-new-habit-66-days.
- Morris, S., 'Domino Chain Reaction (Geometric Growth in Action)', 5 October 2009, https://www.youtube.com/watch?v=y97rBdSYbkg.
- https://en.wikipedia.org/wiki/Anapanasati.

CHAPTER 4

The Law of Resonance: One Catalyst for Holistic Change

- 'Resonance', The Physics Classroom, 30 January 2011, https://www.youtube.com/watch?v=tnS0SYF4pYE.
- LifeVestInside, 'Life Vest Inside—Kindness Boomcrang—"Onc Day"', 30 August 2011, https://www.youtube.com/watch?v=nwAYpLVyeFU.

CHAPTER 6

Small Wins, Small Goals: Unlocking Big Milestones

- Amabile, T.M., and S.J. Kramer, 'The Power of Small Wins', *Harvard Business Review* (May 2011), https://hbr.org/2011/05/the-power-of-small-wins.

CHAPTER 7

Avoiding a Crowd: Strength in Small Teams

- Wang, D., and J.A. Evans, 'Research: When Small Teams Are Better than Big Ones', *Harvard Business Review*,

21 February 2019, https://hbr.org/2019/02/research-when-small-teams-are-better-than-big-ones.

- Mueller, J. S., 'Why Individuals in Larger Teams Perform Worse', Organizational Behavior and Human Decision Processes, *ScienceDirect*, 117(1), pp. 111–124, January 2012, https://doi.org/10.1016/j.obhdp.2011.08.004.

- 'Is Your Team Too Big? Too Small? What's the Right Number?' *Knowledge@Wharton*, The Wharton School, University of Pennsylvania, 14 June 2006, https://knowledge.wharton.upenn.edu/article/is-your-team-too-big-too-small-whats-the-right-number-2/.

CHAPTER 8

Keeping it Short: The Power of Small Meetings

- Doodle, 'The State of Meetings Report 2019', https://assets.ctfassets.net/8t3gydnqcry0/3TLe93eDXOK9jWQ9FpCysE/b660cc2e3f921f601ddc5645548f5472/E-book_-_Meeting_Report_2019.pdf; https://doodle.com/en/resources/research-and-reports-/the-state-of-meetings-2019/.

- Rogelberg, S., 'How to Reap Big Returns from Meetings That Are Just 10 to 15 Minutes Long,' *ideas.ted.com*, 5 September 2019, https://ideas.ted.com/how-to-reap-big-benefits-from-meetings-that-are-just-10-to-15-minutes-long/; Fallarme, D., 'Run Your Meeting like a Boss: Lessons from Mayer, Musk, and Jobs', *99u*, 16 April 2014, https://99u.adobe.com/articles/25075/run-your-meeting-like-a-boss-lessons-from-mayer-musk-and-jobs; Gamelearn Team, 'How to run a meeting like

Marissa Meyer (Yahoo)' *gamelearn*, https://www.game-learn.com/en/resources/blog/how-to-run-a-meeting-like-marissa-mayer-yahoo/

- Brier, N. 'The 6 Meeting Rules of Percolate', *Percolate*, 9 June 2014, https://twitter.com/percolate/status/476033033330368515.
- 'Roombot: Solving Meetings One Room at a Time', *O3*, https://www.o3world.com/labs/roombot/
- Rogelberg S., 'How to Reap Big Returns from Meetings That Are Just 10 to 15 Minutes Long,' *ideas. ted.com*, 5 September 2019, https://ideas.ted.com/how-to-reap-big-benefits-from-meetings-that-are-just-10-to-15-minutes-long/
- 'The Magical Number Seven, Plus or Minus Two', https://en.wikipedia.org/wiki/The_Magical_Number_Seven,_Plus_or_Minus_Two
- Indraksh, A., 'Miller's Law — Is There a Magical Number in UX Design?', *UX Collective*, 28 April 2020, https://uxdesign.cc/millers-law-is-there-a-magical-number-in-ux-design-7999f92ef7b8

CHAPTER 9

Choose Your Niche: Fewer Products, Fewer Problems

- 'Steve Jobs' Advice to Nike: Get Rid of the Crappy Stuff', Fast Company, 16 September 2010, https://www.youtube.com/watch?v=SOCKp9eij3A.

CHAPTER 10

Concise and Captivating: Five Pointers for Crisp Business Presentations

- Phillips, David J.P., 'How to Avoid Death by PowerPoint', TEDxStockholmSalon, 14 April 2014, https://www.youtube.com/watch?v=Iwpi1Lm6dFo.

CHAPTER 12

The Seven Tools of Productivity

- McSpadden, K., 'You Now Have a Shorter Attention Span Than a Goldfish', *TIME*, 14 May 2015, https://time.com/3858309/attention-spans-goldfish/.
- Pangambam, S., 'Steve Jobs iPhone 2007 Presentation (Full Transcript)', *The Singju Post*, 4 July 2014, https://singjupost.com/steve-jobs-iphone-2007-presentation-full-transcript/.
- Cirillo, F., (n.d.). 'The Pomodoro Technique®—proudly developed by Francesco Cirillo', Cirillo Consulting GmbH, https://francescocirillo.com/pages/pomodoro-technique.
- https://www.who.int/teams/integrated-health-services/patient-safety/research/safe-surgery/tool-and-resources.

Epilogue: The Most Important Person

- 'The 3 Most Important Questions to Ask Yourself', Life At MindValley, 3 October 2012, https://www.youtube.com/watch?v=f8eU5Pc-y0g.

THANK YOU

I am very grateful to you for investing your valuable time to read this book. As you harness the source code 'Small is big', fulfilment, productivity and extraordinary results are inevitable.

If this book has inspired you, please share it with others.

Reviews help in informing and inspiring others, so I would request you to write a review on Amazon.

Thank you!

Acknowledgements

The creation of a book is never a stand-alone exercise. It is a creative project where the author seeks inspiration and guidance from several sources. As I reflect on my journey of writing *Small Is Big*, I wish to take a moment and express my gratitude to the special people and experiences that encouraged my pursuit.

On 6 January 2018, I took my first step towards *Small Is Big* when the mysterious Universe sowed its seeds in my mind during an intense meditation experience. The sapling that sprouted from those seeds during my time at the retreat grew into this book. Throughout my voyage, the cosmos found ways to fertilize the sapling and enable its growth. The Universe is like a compassionate mother, looking after us and always ensuring our highest good. I am indebted to its giving nature that has always showed me the way.

As I share my thoughts on how the book came about, I must thank the organizers of the silent meditation programme who provided the platform where I found my inspiration. Thank you very much.

My first book, *The Ultimate Sales Accelerator*, was launched in July 2019. Around five months later, I was in the midst of an interesting conversation with my sons. We were discussing the idea for my second book. *Storytelling*, *Emotional Quotient in Sales* and *Small Is Big* were among the top three title options. Both Tanish and Aarav patiently listened to my thoughts. Without batting an eyelid, they chose the title *Small Is Big* from my suggestions. I still remember Aarav's exact words, 'Daddy, you have to write *Small Is Big*.'

Once again, the Universe inspired me through an unlikely source; my ten- and thirteen-year-old sons! During my conversation with them, my wife Ayesha had been listening to us. When I asked her what she thought should be the title for my second book, she agreed with the kids. That was when I knew for sure that my second book had to be *Small Is Big*.

Ayesha, Tanish and Aarav, thank you for everything. Thank you for your enthusiasm. Thank you for your trust. Above all, thank you for being a part of so many of my life's 'Small is big' experiences. I have shared several of them in the book, and I hope they inspire the community as they have inspired me.

I have always thought of myself as a learner at heart. In January 2020, I was a first-year student in the Dream, Signs and Symbols Interpretation (DSSI) course offered by Universe/City Mikael Teaching and Resource Centre (UCM). UCM is an internationally renowned non-profit organization disseminating knowledge on emotional intelligence, symbolic language and interpretation of dreams. As a part of the DSSI curriculum, I attended a module called 'The Macrocosm in the Microcosm'. Once again, it was a sign from the Universe that invigorated me to continue working on my book *Small Is Big*. Simultaneously, the weekly assignments I had to do for the course were intensely reflective experiences. Through them, I found the chance to work on myself. For these vital inputs and for the many transformative opportunities during the course, I am grateful to my UCM teachers. Thank you very much, Professor Kaya, Professor Christiane, Professor Eloi, Professor Santosh and the entire DSSI support team.

From January 2020 to June 2020, I attempted to weave the concept of 'Small is big' into every aspect of my life. Many thoughts were running through my mind: How do I succinctly express the all-pervasive nature of 'Small is big' in one book? How do I demonstrate the principles of 'Small is big' in the personal, professional and spiritual contexts?

I began writing down all my observations in the Keep My Notes application on my phone. Every note I made reinforced my belief that Small is indeed Big, and that the source code can be applied to make our lives happier. In addition to notes, one of the most beneficial tools that helped structure my ideas was mind maps. I drew mind maps for the book on 2 July 2020, and during the writing process I built many more. They helped me gain excellent clarity in shaping the book. For creating and evangelizing such a fantastic tool, I am grateful to Tony Buzan, the inventor of mind maps. In this book, I have highlighted seven productivity tools aligned with the 'Small is big' source code. Mind maps is one of them.

Since July 2020, every morning, from 5.30 to 7.30, I worked on *Small Is Big*. This time is often referred to as *Brahma Mahurat,* or the Holy Hour. Starting work daily at 5.30 a.m. sounds quite hard to sustain, right? How I cultivated and held on to this habit is indeed a fascinating story in itself. In 2018, I read a life-changing book called *The One Thing*, which made me ask the following question: *What's the one habit I can develop in 2018, such that by developing it, everything else will be easier or unnecessary?*

My answer was, 'Waking up at 5 a.m.' Joining the 5 a.m. club allowed me to find the perfect time to concentrate on my book and to write it. For initiating this life-changing habit, I thank the writers of *The One Thing,* Gary W. Keller and Jay Papasan. At the same time, I am grateful to Robin Sharma for evangelizing the 5 a.m. movement; I absorbed it subconsciously and found it the most appropriate habit to form after I read *The One Thing*.

My second book is in a terrain entirely different from my first. It has been rewarding and yet challenging, on more than one count. To traverse this new terrain, I required a calm mind. Here, practising Vipassana was of immense benefit. During meditation and sleep, I received many insights. Thank you, Lord Buddha, for this valuable and deeply impactful gift of Vipassana, and thank you, Shri S.N. Goenka Ji, for sharing it with others.

Tahseen, Vidisha and Suman are three angels who need special mention.

Amidst the pandemic and work pressure, Tahseen found the time to read and review the first draft of the manuscript and provided valuable feedback. What was even more heartening was how she implemented a few principles from *Small Is Big* in her life. Thank you, Tahseen, for your time and input.

Vidisha did exemplary work in editing and refining the manuscript over two and a half months. This book has three sections, and they can be considered three different books. Vidisha gave superb support in ensuring that each section is connected to the other. When you read the book, you will realize how each thought, unit and chapter is closely interlinked with the others. I remember having tears in my eyes after reading the refined manuscript in February 2021. Thank you, Vidisha, for your wonderful help in editing the book and reviewing its contents from a reader's perspective.

Throughout the book, you will notice many visuals that help convey the various concepts. I am grateful to Suman for creating visuals and illustrations for these.

In March 2021, amidst the pandemic, I began reaching out to publishers. Given the circumstances, I was not sure how long it would take. Interestingly, the Universe guided me to Atul Jalan, CEO of Algonomy, who referred me to Penguin Random House. Thank you so much, Atul.

I vividly recollect my first interaction with Radhika, my commissioning editor at the publishing house. I remember her enthusiasm as she listened to the pitch for the book. My heartfelt gratitude to her and to the entire team for believing in *Small Is Big* and publishing it. Thanks to Akangksha for her exemplary work in designing the book cover. Thanks to Ralph and Kripa for their support in copy-editing the manuscript. Working with the entire Penguin team was wonderful. Thank you, Team Penguin.

Finally, I would like to express my earnest appreciation for my readers. You have subconsciously inspired me to write this book. I love the saying, 'There is no friend more loyal than a book', and I hope this book serves you as a loyal friend.

Thank you,
Amit Agarwal